Understanding Privacy and Data Protection

What You Need to Know

Timothy J. Toohey

ACKNOWLEDGMENT

I acknowledge the support and assistance of my colleagues, Marc Currie, Jennifer Dioguardi, Kevin Jackson, Pat Fowler, Joan Macneil, Seepan Parseghian, Matt Schoonover, Stan Stahl, and Becky Winterscheidt.

Particular kudos to Gregory Ge and Sean Mossman for providing valuable research for several chapters of the book.

DEDICATION

This book is dedicated to the memory of my parents and with gratitude to David Liu, who continues to encourage my work in this rapidly developing and challenging field.

CONTENTS

Contents

Introduction

Consider a day in your highly connected life. As always, the first thing you do when you get up in the morning is check your e-mail. Today you receive an e-mail from a manufacturer of a home security camera you recently bought to monitor your baby telling you that a security flaw in the camera has allowed a hacker to post pictures of your baby on the Internet with information about your location obtained from your computer's IP address. Needless to say, you are very upset.

You also receive an unpleasant shock when you check a social networking website and find that personal and potentially embarrassing information that you posted is available for everyone to see. You are worried about your boss's reaction, but the website refuses to take down the post, saying you agreed to make it public.

Rattled by these developments, you leave for work. When you get to the office, you are irritated to receive yet another text message from a fast food company application that you installed on your phone to get a discount coupon. You immediately text a "STOP" message to the mobile app and are upset to receive a confirmatory text message saying you are unsubscribed.

An employee, who has just returned to her job, complains that you have been using her Twitter password in her absence to post tweets. You explain that the account belongs to the company, not the employee personally, but she threatens to sue your company for breach of privacy. Matters go from bad to worse when your IT manager tells you that a group of "hactivists" have attacked the company's website with a Distributed Denial of Service (DDoS) attack and that the website is off line for the foreseeable future.

Shaken by the day's developments, you arrive home to see on the evening news that Russian hackers have taken advantage of a social network's poor password protection policies to gain administrative access to the site and have stolen millions of unencrypted user passwords. You locate your LinkedIn password on an infamous hacker website and realize that you use the same password for your bank, PayPal, and numerous other sites. In a panic, you change your passwords before going to bed.

Perhaps an improbable series of events for a single day, but these incidents illustrate the dangers we all face in a world where the Internet both links us and disperses our personal information seemingly beyond our control. In the environment in which we live, privacy and data security concerns are a great unifier. The personal and proprietary information of consumers, employees, children, employers, business enterprises, and even the government may be attacked and exposed. Information that once would have been difficult to uncover is now a click away for hostile actors. Our reputations, assets, and identity are vulnerable and subject to almost constant attack by hackers, criminals, and state-sponsored actors.

The incidents described are not theoretical. Each is based (with some modification) on an actual privacy or security event and most led to lawsuits by the injured parties. In the camera security flaw case, the Federal Trade Commission (FTC) brought claims against the manufacturer, Trendnet, under the Federal Trade Act's prohibition of unfair and deceptive trade practices.[1] The plaintiff in the lawsuit where personal information was posted on the Internet sued the Internet Movie Database (IMDb) for breach of contract and violation of state privacy and consumer protection laws for revealing her age.[2] The plaintiff in the unwanted text message case charged that his rights were violated by a Taco Bell franchise under the Telephone Consumer Protection Act's restriction of unsolicited telemarketing calls.[3] The employee alleging misuse of her Twitter password brought claims for trademark infringement, violation of the Stored Communications Act, and state right

---

[1] Press Release, Federal Trade Commission, *Marketer of Internet-Connected Home Security Video Cameras Settles FTC Charges It Failed to Protect Consumer' Privacy*, Sept. 4, 2013, http://www.ftc.gov/opa/2013/09/trendnet.shtm.

[2] *Privacy on Trial: Reflections on Hoang v. IMDb*, TECHNOLOGY & MARKETING Blog April 11, 2013, http://blog.ericgoldman.org/archives/2013/04/privacy_on_tria_1.htm.

[3] *Confirmatory Opt-Out Text Message Doesn't Violate TCPA - Ibey v. Taco Bell*, TECHNOLOGY & MARKETING LAW BLOG, Jul. 6, 2012, http://blog.ericgoldman.org/archives/2012/07/confirmatory_op.htm.

of publicity laws against her employer.[4] The plaintiffs in the lawsuits against LinkedIn sued for unfair competition, breach of contract, and for breach of an implied agreement to reasonably safeguard user information.[5]

Despite the fact that privacy impacts so many aspects of our interconnected lives, these lawsuits show that, unlike some other countries, there is no single comprehensive US data privacy law. In addition to the laws used in these cases, separate federal laws govern health care, financial services, information about children, and unauthorized access to computers. These laws are supplemented by hundreds of state laws that govern reporting security breaches, privacy policies, credit reports, social security numbers, and confidentiality of personal information. The United States thus relies on what is sometimes called a "patchwork quilt" of federal and state laws, many of which have not kept up with technological change or were not originally written with privacy concerns in mind.

Anyone attempting to navigate the privacy maze confronts further complications. Self-governing standards and best practices, including the commitments businesses make in their posted privacy policies, apply to many critical privacy and security practices, but are not mandated by law. Businesses that send information outside this country or have employees abroad must comply not only with US laws, but also with international laws that are frequently inconsistent with those in this country. Perpetual technological change affects privacy practices and expectations and requires businesses almost constantly to update their internal processes and procedures. Finally, because of rapid change and unsettled legal standards, privacy expectations of both businesses and consumers may be out of step with the existing state of the law, which further complicates risk management and best practices.

---

[4] Venkat Balasumbramani, *Employee's claims against employer for unauthorized use of social media accounts move forward - Maremont v. S.F. Design Group, Ltd., et al.*, TECHNOLOGY & MARKETING BLOG, Dec. 8, 2011, http://blog.ericgoldman.org/archives/2011/12/maremont_v_sfg.htm.
[5] Venkat Balasumbramani, *Court dismisses data breach lawsuit against Linkedin based on comprised passwords – In re Linkedin User Privacy Litigation*, http://blog.ericgoldman.org/archives/2013/03/court_dismisses_7.htm; *see also* Chenda Ngak, CBS News, *6.5 Million LinkedIn Passwords Reportedly Leaked on Russian Hacker Site*, June 6, 2012, http://www.cbsnews.com/8301-501465_162-57448222-501465/6.5-million-linkedin-passwords-reportedly-leaked-on-russian-hacker-site/.

Despite the complexities of the field, it is more than ever important for consumers and businesses alike to understand the legal framework and ongoing trends affecting privacy and data security. As shown by the "day in the life" episode that opens this chapter, privacy and data security can affect almost every aspect of our digital world. Public opinion polls also show that consumers value privacy and take efforts to guard it, even though we are sharing more and more information online. These polls show that consumers prefer businesses that protect and secure information and that privacy is an increasingly important value for consumers.[6]

Privacy also impacts data flow, which is the life blood for many vital business functions. Enterprises collect and store data of all sorts in large amounts, including personal and business proprietary information. They depend upon their ability to use, transfer, and retain data for crucial marketing functions and tailor advertising by using personal data provided by consumers. The failure to respect privacy and security may therefore result in significant financial loss, lawsuits, fines, and considerable reputational harm.

As the opening scenario also shows, data privacy is at the heart of communications and services that are a necessary and accustomed part of our daily life. We provide personal information in return for free services, including search engines and social networks. We communicate via e-mails, texts, social media, and tweets. For many of us, the exchange of personal information for free services is natural and unremarkable. But for others, the collection and customization of personal information raises concerns akin to the dystopian worlds of George Orwell's *1984* or Steven Spielberg's *Minority Report*, where even the shoes we wear and the cars we drive are communicating information about our movements to others.

Collection and analysis of personal data can also reveal unexpected patterns that, depending upon one's point of view, are either beneficial or disconcerting. On the beneficial side, researchers using data mining techniques on anonymous Internet search histories and the Food and Drug Administration's Adverse Event Reporting System have found

---

[6] Ponemon Institute, *2012 Most Trusted Companies for Privacy*, 1-2, Jan. 28, 2013, http://www.ponemon.org/local/upload/file/2012%20MTC%20Report%20FINAL.pdf.

unexpected drug interactions that would have been difficult to discern from traditional structured databases.[7]

On the disconcerting side, a large national store used data gleaned through electronic tracking of purchases to find those purchases that predict whether a shopper was likely to be pregnant. Using these findings, the store sent women who had made such purchases coupons for baby items and maternity clothes. This produced some interesting reactions, as when a father complained that his teenage daughter had improperly received coupons, only to find out that his daughter was in fact pregnant.[8]

Misuse of personal data creates significant security headaches. To take one example, a writer for *Wired* reported that in the course of an hour hackers seeking access to his Twitter handle gained access to his Apple account to wipe out his iPhone, iPad, and MacBook, "deleting all my messages and documents and every picture I'd ever taken of my 18-month old daughter."[9] Concerned with the vulnerability of private information in a world with imperfect security, he found that "[w]ith two minutes and $4 to spend at a sketchy foreign website, I could report back with your credit card, phone, and Social Security Numbers and your home address. Allow me five minutes more and I could be inside your accounts for, say, Amazon, Best Buy, Hulu, Microsoft, and Netflix. With yet 10 more, I could take over your AT&T, Comcast and Verizon [accounts]. Give me 20—total—and I own your PayPal."

Businesses also have suffered an onslaught of crippling attacks. A group calling itself the Syrian Electronic Army brought down the website of the *New York Times* for nearly two days with a DDoS attack. Cyberattacks have grown so rapidly that the agent in charge of the FBI's cyber branch in New York has

---

[7] Sarah C. P. Williams, *Mining consumers' web searches can reveal unreported side effects of drugs, researchers say*, Stanford School of Medicine, Mar. 6, 2013, http://med.stanford.edu/ism/2013/march/altman.html.

[8] Charles Duhigg, *How Companies Learn Your Secrets*, N.Y. TIMES, Feb. 16, 2012, http://www.nytimes.com/2012/02/19/magazine/shopping-habits.html?pagewanted=1&_r=2&hp&.

[9] Mat Honan, *Kill the Password: Why a String of Characters Can't Protect Us Anymore*, WIRED, Nov. 15, 2012, http://www.wired.com/gadgetlab/2012/11/ff-mat-honan-password-hacker/all/.

said that there are only two types of companies—"Those companies that have been hacked, and those that are going to be hacked again."[10]

Cyberattacks exact enormous costs. A July 2013 study of the economic effect of cybercrime and cyber espionage estimates the expense of cybersecurity attacks in the United States at as much as $120 billion. Another 2013 study put the average total organizational cost of a data breach in the United States at $5,403,644. It is therefore not surprising that a 2012 survey of general counsel and CEOs at major corporations for the first time ranked cybersecurity as their number one concern—ahead of perils such as natural disasters or reputational harm to the business.

Privacy and cybersecurity issues may even affect international relations. In early 2013, the *New York Times* ran a story highlighting that the Chinese military was allegedly behind many attacks on private businesses and the US government. Edward Snowden's revelation of surveillance activities by the National Security Agency (NSA) also threatened to cause a diplomatic rift with some US allies that may affect the ability of companies to transfer data from the European Union (EU) to the United States.

Data privacy and security issues that once were the province of geeks and a small cadre of cybersecurity lawyers now feature almost daily in the news. But despite widespread publicity, privacy continues to be controversial in some quarters. Silicon Valley executives have declared that privacy is dead because people so freely share private information online in return for free services. Focusing on national security, others claim that personal privacy must be sacrificed to protect ourselves against internal and external threats in the post 9/11 world. Some critics see privacy as inimical to the First Amendment, claiming that the right to know should trump the right to keep information private.

Despite these controversies, privacy and data security will continue to be important topics for consumers and businesses in our digital world. Recognizing the importance of the issues, this book goes beyond the headlines to explore the context of existing laws, as well as ongoing trends and technological developments that will continue to have a practical effect on privacy expectations and best practices.

---

[10] Andrew Tangel, *FBI Agent Austin Berglas Fights Cyberattacks on Corporate America*, L.A. TIMES, Sept. 21, 2013, http://www.latimes.com/business/la-fi-0921-fbi-cyber-qa-2013 0921,0,3321489.story.

After providing a short history of the field and a description of the major stakeholders, this book outlines the important federal and state laws pertaining to data privacy and security in the United States, including laws affecting specific business sectors, such as finance and health care, and types of information, such as data regarding children. Although it is not possible to discuss every aspect of these laws, Chapters 2 and 3 provide an overview of the federal and state laws that businesses and consumers are most likely to encounter.

Because data is often sent outside the United States in digital form, Chapter 4 discusses major data and privacy laws in North America, Europe, Asia, and Australia. Understanding these laws is important not only for companies that engage in cross-border transfers of personal information, but for appreciating the differences between the sectoral protections and self-regulatory regime prevailing in the United States and the more proscriptive approach of other countries.

Privacy in the workplace is discussed in Chapter 5. The blurring of the lines between home and work and technological developments, such as social media, challenge both employers and employees. The chapter therefore focuses on battleground issues affecting privacy and security, including social media use, "Bring Your Own Device" (BYOD), and the ability of employers to control employees' use of technology.

Companies are responsible for data breaches, even if they consider themselves the victims of such attacks. Cybersecurity also presents considerable operational challenges for personal and proprietary data because of the exponential increase in cyberattacks. Chapter 6 discusses these security issues, including corporate liability for breaches imposed by federal and state law, data breach notification laws, and self-governing codes and standards.

Enforcement of privacy law by the government and private parties is addressed not only because it poses business challenges, but because it is an important aspect of the US privacy ecosystem. Chapter 7 addresses the FTC's enforcement of privacy and security laws, highlighting prominent recent cases demonstrating the range of the commission's powers and enforcement priorities. Chapter 8 focuses on another side of enforcement—litigation by private parties against businesses, primarily in the technology sector.

An emerging issue affecting data privacy and security is the 2013 controversy over government surveillance discussed in Chapter 9. Although government surveillance is qualitatively different from collection of information by private parties, the controversy over the NSA programs affects privacy expectations about the collection and retention by businesses of large amounts of personal data.

Chapter 10 addresses technological developments, including "cloud computing," biometric identifiers, "Big Data," and the "Internet of Things." As new technologies arise, so do new privacy challenges. Businesses adopting new technologies must constantly modify their policies and procedures, including the privacy policies used to communicate privacy and security practices to consumers, so they do not cause privacy harms or suffer security breaches.

Chapter 11 provides practical suggestions for dealing with key emerging issues in the privacy and data security world. Although no "one size fits all" solution is possible, approaches that may prove useful include developing internal policies and procedures; best practices for privacy policies; infrastructure and corporate organizational structures for privacy and security personnel; privacy and security audits; managing vendors and third parties; incorporating "privacy by design" principles into business organization and operations; and obtaining cybersecurity insurance to manage risk.

* * *

Frequent use of acronyms may make books on privacy and data security resemble tangled alphabet soup. Although the book tries to minimize their use, a table of frequently used abbreviations is included immediately after the Introduction.

Given the limitations of space and the complexity and evolving nature of the subject, it is impossible to outline every aspect of the privacy and security laws mentioned here. This book is also not intended to convey legal advice about any law or legal provision mentioned nor should it be construed as such. Because privacy and data security are technical matters impacted by constantly changing legal standards, those with specific problems or questions should consult counsel experienced in the field. I have tried to present fairly the views of the clashing sides in the controversies discussed, but any views expressed are mine alone and do not reflect the views of the law firm with which I am associated.

Commonly Used Abbreviations

ACLU	American Civil Liberties Union
APEC	Asia-Pacific Economic Cooperation
BYOD	Bring Your Own Device
CalOPPA	California Online Privacy Protection Act
CFAA	Computer Fraud and Abuse Act
CIO	Chief Information Officer
CIPA	California Invasion of Privacy Act
CISPA	Cyber Intelligence Sharing and Protection Act
CMIA	California Medical Information Act
COPPA	Children's Online Privacy Protection Act
CPO	Chief Privacy Officer
CSO	Chief Security Officer
DNT	Do Not Track (technology)
DPA	Data Protection Authority
ECPA	Electronic Communications Protection Act
EPIC	Electronic Privacy Information Center
EU	European Union
FCRA	Fair Credit Reporting Act
FIPPs	Fair Information Practice Principles
FISA	Foreign Intelligence Surveillance Act
FISC	Foreign Intelligence Surveillance Court
FTC	Federal Trade Commission
FTC Act	Federal Trade Commission Act
GLB	Gramm-Leach-Bliley (also known as Financial Services Modernization Act)
HIPAA	Health Information Portability and Accountability Act
HITECH	Health Information Technology for Economic and Clinical Health
IoT	The Internet of Things
NIST	National Institute of Standards and Technology (Department of Commerce)
NLRB	National Labor Relations Board
NSA	National Security Agency
OBA	Online Behavioral Advertising

NSA	National Security Agency
PCI DSS	Payment Card Industry Data Security Standards
SCA	Stored Communications Act
SEC	Securities and Exchange Commission
SOX	Sarbanes Oxley Act
SSN	Social Security Number
TCPA	Telephone Communications Protection Act

1

Data Privacy

"Privacy" is a word in frequent daily use in our society, but the term "data privacy" has a specialized meaning closely linked to the legal protection of personal information maintained and shared through computerized technology. When governments and businesses began to use networked computers in the 1960s, worries arose that the technology would lead to the loss of personal privacy and the compilation of computerized "dossiers." To address these concerns, a US government committee formulated fair information principles to give people rights over their computerized personal information.

With the greater connectivity allowed by the growth of the Internet, government authorities began to express new concerns about the appropriate protection of personal data in a world where information is shared and persists indefinitely. These concerns led to legislation for some business sectors and types of information. As additional laws have been proposed, privacy stakeholders continue to debate the tradeoff between free Internet services and the privacy of personal data in an interlinked digital society.

The Many Meanings of "Privacy"

In one of the most influential law review articles ever published, Samuel D. Warren and future US Supreme Court Justice Louis D. Brandeis in 1890 posited that the right to privacy is the "right to be left alone."[1] Concerned in

---

[1] Samuel D. Warren & Louis D. Brandeis, *The Right to Privacy*, 5 HARV. L. REV. 193 (1890).

part with the rise of inexpensive photographic technology, Warren and Brandeis called for increased protection of personal information from prying eyes—particularly the press. In the years after the article, the United States developed legal protections for some aspects of personal privacy and began allowing lawsuits based on a variety of privacy harms, including public disclosure of private facts that a reasonable person would find objectionable or highly offensive, intrusion of solitude, and unauthorized appropriation of a person's name or likeness.

Once expressed in terms of the right to be left alone, privacy has now come to have many meanings. In recent years, a "taxonomy" of privacy has been proposed with four main parts—"information collection," "information processing," "information dissemination," and "invasion." "Information collection" includes practices such as government surveillance and interrogation. "Information processing" comprises aggregation of data, identity theft, and the right of data subjects to know about data processing. Under "information dissemination" falls breach of confidentiality, disclosure of private information, exposure of the physical and emotional attributes of a person, and blackmail. "Invasion" is intrusion into the home and interference with decisions, such as the right to use contraception.[2]

Some reject the effort to define privacy, claiming that the term only has meaning in its social context.[3] Others contend that privacy is overused or overrated and at odds with the unrestricted access of information necessary for a free market economy and First Amendment freedoms. In an interconnected world where people willingly share private information on the Internet, prominent voices in Silicon Valley have even proclaimed the death of privacy. Mark Zuckerberg of Facebook has said that the age of privacy is over.[4] Scott McNealy, the former CEO of Sun Microsystems, famously said, "You have zero privacy anyway....Get over it."[5] Reid Hoffman, the founder of social networking site LinkedIn,

---

[2] DANIEL J. SOLOVE, UNDERSTANDING PRIVACY 101-70 (Harvard University Press, 2008).

[3] FRED CATE, PRIVACY IN THE INFORMATION AGE 22 (Brookings Institution, 1997).

[4] Marshall Kirkpatrick, *Facebook's Zuckerberg Says The Age of Privacy is Over*, READWRITE, Jan. 9, 2010, http://readwrite.com/2010/01/09/facebooks_zuckerberg_ says_the_age_of_ privacy_is_ov.

[5] Polly Sprenger, *Sun on Privacy: 'Get Over It,'* WIRED, Jan. 26, 1999, http://www.wired. com/politics/law/news/1999/01/17538.

also proclaimed that "all these concerns about privacy tend to be old people issues."[6]

It is fortunately possible to discuss the privacy of personal data without resolving philosophical or legal debates about the meaning of the term "privacy." Except for a discussion of the effect of government surveillance on data privacy, this book concentrates on "data privacy" and the activities of private or commercial enterprises. A working definition of the term as it is used here comes from Alan Westin, who wrote that the privacy of data rests on the "'claim of individuals, groups, or institutions to determine for themselves when, how, and to what extent information about them is communicated to others.'"[7]

Personal Data

Personal data can be defined both generally and specifically. The EU has a general definition of "personal data" in its 1995 Data Protection Directive as "any information relating to an identified or identifiable natural person." An "identifiable person" is defined as "one who can be identified, directly or indirectly, in particular by reference to an identification number or to one or more factors specific to his physical, physiological, mental, economic, cultural or social identity."[8]

A more specific definition of the related term "personal information" comes from the latest revision of the Children's Online Privacy Protection Rule (COPPA), which became effective on July 1, 2013. Under this definition, personal information consists of:

- First and last name;
- A home or other physical address including street name and name of a city or town;

[6] World Economic Forum Video, *Davos Annual Meeting 2010 – The Growing Influence of Social Networks*, Jan. 27, 2010, http://www.youtube.com/watch?v=pexGCUPlUe A&feature=player_embedded.

[7] *See Cate supra* n. 3, *quoting* ALAN F. WESTIN, PRIVACY AND FREEDOM 7 (Bodley Head Ltd, 1967).

[8] 1995 O.J. (L 281/31), Directive 95/46/EC, art. 2(a), (European Parliament & Council of 24 October 1995 on the protection of individuals regard to the processing of personal data and on the free movement of such data) [hereinafter EU Directive], *available at* http://ec.europa.eu/justice/policies/privacy/docs/95-46-ce/dir1995-46_part1_en.pdf.

- Online contact information;
- A screen or user name that functions as online contact information;
- A telephone number;
- A social security number;
- A persistent identifier that can be used to recognize a user over time and across different websites or online services;
- A photograph, video, or audio file, where such file contains a child's image or voice;
- Geolocation information sufficient to identify street name and name of a city or town; or
- Information concerning the child or the parents of the child that the operator collects online from the child and combines with an identifier described above.[9]

Common definitions of "personal information" (or "personally identifiable information" (PII) as it is sometimes called) are found in other state and federal laws. Under the California law requiring notification to consumers for data breaches, "personal information" includes a person's first name or first initial and last name in combination with a social security number, driver's license or identification card number, account number, credit or debit card number in combination with required security or access code, medical information or health insurance information.[10] Other definitions of personal information are found in regulations and standards discussed in later chapters of this book.

Evolution of Data Privacy

Fair Information Practice Principles (FIPPs)

Privacy laws based on the right to be left alone arising in the late nineteenth century and early twentieth century were stimulated in part by the development of personal cameras. The fear that "fiendish Kodakers" were "lying in wait" to snap photos of private occasions that would be

---

[9] Federal Trade Commission, *Complying with COPPA Frequently Asked Questions*, revised Jul. 2013, [hereinafter "Complying with COPPA"], http://business.ftc.gov/documents/Complying-with-COPPA-Frequently-Asked-Questions.
[10] Ann. Cal. Civ. Code § 1798.82(h) (West).

displayed in the popular press prompted a concern for greater privacy protections.[11] Later technological advancements, such as the telephone, led to a debate over the constitutionality of wiretapping that lasted several decades. More recently, the growth of networked computing prompted the development of a set of comprehensive data privacy principles called the Fair Information Practice Principles (FIPPs) that continue to act as a framework for data privacy expectations and rights.

The FIPPs date to a 1973 report of a Special Advisory Committee to the US Secretary of Health, Education and Welfare created in response to the concerns of scientists, lawyers, and politicians that the increasing use of networked computers was allowing compilation of individual "dossiers" of personal information that were endangering personal autonomy and producing automated decision making with little or no human input.

As early as 1967, Paul Baran of the RAND Corporation, who is credited with the idea of "packet switching" on which the modern Internet is based, said that the "automation of information flow" across computer networks was putting people at a significant disadvantage in protecting their personal data from businesses and the government. As Baran wrote, "[w]e can no longer count on the protection we give our own files. All our information will be stored elsewhere."[12] (The worry about dossiers is resilient, as is seen by the ACLU's current objection to the compilation by the government of "vast dossiers about innocent people" that sit "indefinitely in government databases . . .")[13]

The FIPPs arose out of efforts by interested persons, including Baran's fellow RAND scientist Willis Ware, to address the drawbacks people face in protecting their personal information in a computerized age. Ware, who sat on the committee that developed the principles, states that the FIPPs were formulated to "adjust the balance of power between citizen and record system in such fashion that the individual has both

---

[11] JEFF JARVIS, PUBLIC PARTS 63-5 (Simon & Schuster, 2011).
[12] Paul Baran, *The Coming Computer Utility: Laissez-Faire, Licensing or Regulation?* 9-10 (The Rand Institute, Apr. 1967). A somewhat modified version of this paper was published as Paul Baran, *The future computer utility,* 8 PUBLIC INTEREST 75 (1967).
[13] American Civil Liberties Union, *Surveillance and Privacy,* http://www.aclu.org/national-security/surveillance-privacy.

opportunity and a mechanism to contest, correct and control personal information held about himself."[14]

The FIPPs have proved to be enduring. As reformulated by the FTC in 1998 as "fair information principles," they call for compliance with basic principles of notice, choice, access, and security.[15] People should be given advance notice about data that is collected about them, including information and choice about how that data is used; options about how the data is to be used and a means to prevent the data from being used for purposes other than those for which it was collected; the ability to access, correct, and amend the data; and assurances that data be kept securely. The FTC also suggested in its 1998 report that consumers be given a means of redress if the principles are breached.

An anomaly of US privacy law is that the FIPPs have never been embodied in comprehensive privacy legislation governing data collection and processing by businesses. As discussed in the next chapter, the United States, unlike some other countries, including the member states of the EU, has adopted privacy laws only for certain business sectors, such as health care and financial services, and has resisted a comprehensive or "baseline" privacy law.

Despite the lack of a comprehensive privacy law, data privacy discussions are still often framed in terms of the FIPPs. In 2012, the White House and the FTC proposed strengthening privacy protections in the United States by closing the gaps created by sectoral laws through adoption of principles owing much to the FIPPs. In its proposal for a "Consumer Privacy Bill of Rights," the White House called for establishing consumer rights for online privacy based on individual control, transparency, respect for context, security, access and accuracy, focused collection, and accountability.[16] The FTC similarly cited simplified consumer choice and

---

[14] Willis Ware, *Records, Computers and the Rights of Citizens*, 2, Aug. 1973.

[15] Federal Trade Commission, *Privacy Online: A Report to Congress*, 7-11, June 1998, [hereinafter FTC 1998 Report], http://www.ftc.gov/reports/privacy3/priv-23a.pdf; *see also* Federal Trade Commission, *Privacy Online: Fair Information Practices in the Electronic Marketplace: A Report to Congress* (May 2000) [hereinafter FTC 2000 Report], http://www.ftc.gov/reports/privacy2000/privacy2000.pdf.

[16] The White House, *Consumer Data Privacy in a Networked World: A Framework for Protecting Privacy and Promoting Innovation in the Global Digital Economy* 1 (Feb.

transparency of businesses' data practices as key aspects of its proposal to increase privacy protection.[17]

The Internet Era

Emerging at the birth of networked computing in the 1960s, data privacy achieved greater prominence in the Internet era of the 1990s. As personal computers were connected to the Internet, opportunities to publicly share information that in the past might have remained private grew exponentially. The Internet also produced concerns that people would not be able to control the distribution and use of their personal data. As Jeffrey Rosen wrote in the *New York Times*, "[t]he fact that the Internet never seems to forget is threatening, at an almost existential level, our ability to control our identities; to preserve the option of reinventing ourselves and starting anew; to overcome our checkered pasts."[18]

For its visionaries, the Internet is above all an open system—a "world in which most goods and services are free or practically free, thereby liberating the individuals to pursue self-expression and self-actualization as an activity of primary importance."[19] But for its critics, the Internet poses significant privacy dangers because users lack control over personal information that can be digitally distributed (and redistributed) worldwide and stored in numerous locations. The Internet gives people useful services, such as social networking sites and search engines, but also produces privacy concerns and challenges.

Data Privacy Stakeholders

To understand the trends that continue to affect privacy law, it is necessary to identify some key players.

2012) [hereinafter White House 2012 Report], http://www.whitehouse.gov/sites/default/files/privacy-final.pdf.

[17] Federal Trade Commission, *Protecting Consumer Privacy in an Era of Rapid Change: Recommendations for Businesses and Policymakers* I, Mar. 2012, [hereinafter FTC 2012 Report], http://ftc.gov/os/2012/03/120326privacyreport.pdf.

[18] Jeffrey Rosen, *The Web Means the End of Forgetting*, N.Y. TIMES, Jul. 21, 2010, http://www.nytimes.com/2010/07/25/magazine/25privacy-t2.html?pagewanted=all&_r=0.

[19] TIM WU, THE MASTER SWITCH: THE RISE AND FALL OF INFORMATION EMPIRES 296 (Vintage Press 2011).

Prominent on the "pro-privacy" side are consumer advocacy organizations, including the American Civil Liberties Union (ACLU), the Electronic Privacy Information Center (EPIC), and the Electronic Frontier Foundation (EFF). These and other consumer advocates believe that people should have greater rights to control their personal information and call for legislation to restrict businesses' collection and use of such information. To cite one instance, EPIC has called for a "Do Not Track" (DNT) option on browsers to inhibit targeted advertising because "[t]he general public has very little idea that every second they are on the Internet, their behavior is being tracked and used to create a 'profile' which is then sold to companies on 'stock-market-like exchanges.'"[20]

Countering these organizations are businesses advocating relatively unrestricted exchange of personal data in return for consumers' free access to information and Internet services. These businesses and their advocates believe that the free flow of data is vital to the Internet and that greater privacy restrictions would inhibit innovation and stifle economic growth. The advertising industry thus opposes DNT as a default on browsers because it would "take the information out of the information economy" and destroy the Internet, which is the "symbol of the United States' famed innovation, ingenuity, inventiveness, and entrepreneurial spirit."[21] US Internet companies have also lobbied on similar grounds against increasing privacy protection both in the European Union and in the United States.

Consumer attitudes are less well defined. A 2012 survey found that 68 percent of Americans dislike targeted advertising and 59 percent see the business practice of targeting ads based on data collected from users of e-mail, search or social networking sites as an "unjustified use of private information." However, 56 percent of those surveyed do not want the government to get more involved in how Internet companies handle privacy issues and only 38 percent say the government should be more active.[22] The statistics for mobile applications are similar with 69 percent

---

[20] Electronic Privacy Information Center, *Online Tracking and Behavioral Profiling*, http://epic.org/privacy/consumer/online_tracking_and_behavioral.html.
[21] Association of National Advertisers, *Letter from Association of National Advertisers (ANA) to Steve Ballmer, CEO of Microsoft*, Oct. 1, 2012, *available at* http://www.ana.net/content/show/id/analetter-microsoft.
[22] Pew Internet Survey, *Search Engine Use 2012*, Mar. 9, 2012, http://www.pewinternet.org/

of users disliking ad tracking, 28 percent neither liking nor disliking it, and only 3 percent liking it.[23]

Congress has divided views with some members siding with the advertising industry and Internet companies and others with consumer organizations. The Obama Administration has been relatively pro-privacy, threatening to veto a cybersecurity bill passed by the House of Representatives that it claimed did not provide adequate privacy protections. The White House's proposed Consumer Privacy Bill of Rights also seeks to balance the benefits that consumers receive from Internet services with privacy protections. Recognizing that "personal data fuels an advertising marketplace that brings many online services and sources of content to consumers free," the White House's proposal nonetheless called for greater consumer protection "from intrusions by both private and governmental actors."[24] Complicating the debate, as will be discussed in Chapter 9, is the controversy over government surveillance, which has affected views about the gathering and retention of large amounts of personal data.

Self-Governance

The next chapters address numerous US privacy and data security laws. Besides these laws, however, many companies in the United States have adopted self-regulatory measures by way of internal policies and procedures. For example, laws may not require specific security measures, but instead allow a business to adopt its own "reasonable" protections, which are then set out in a company's internal policies and procedures. Companies may also adopt contractually required standards such as the Payment Card Industry Data Security Standards, voluntary standards, such as VeriSign authentication services for websites or the Digital Advertising Alliance's self-regulatory program for online behavioral advertising, or privacy management services, such as those

Reports/2012/Search-Engine-Use-2012/Summary-of-findings.aspx; *see also* Pew Research Center for the People & the Press, *Auto Bailout Now Backed, Stimulus Divisive* (Chapter on Privacy and Government Regulations) (Feb. 23, 2012), http://www.people-press.org/2012/02/23/auto-bailout-now-backed-stimulus-divisive/?src=prc-headline.
[23] TRUSTe Privacy Index, *2013 Consumer Data Privacy Study-Mobile Edition*, https://www.privacyassociation.org/media/pdf/knowledge_center/US_ConsumerData_Mobile_FINAL.pdf.
[24] *See* White House 2012 Report *supra* n. 16 at 5.

offered by TRUSTe.[25] These self-regulatory procedures are difficult to catalog, but nonetheless play an important part in the privacy ecosystem.

Several reasons exist for the prevalence of self-governance in the United States. For some of its proponents, self-regulation promotes free market values, including consumer choice and competition. In the view of such free market advocates, self-regulation is preferable to proscriptive comprehensive laws and the bureaucracy of data protection authorities. In opposing privacy restrictions for online marketing, a FTC Commissioner recently said that "[a]dvertising—however tasteless and excessive it might sometime seem—is useful information. The free flow of commercial information is indispensable."[26]

Others resist European-style comprehensive privacy laws because they see them as ineffective. Lothar Determann, who teaches data privacy law both in Europe and the United States, said that it is a "myth" that European laws are better than those in the United States because of the "historic lack of enforcement of data protection laws in Europe."[27] That the "most meaningful innovation in the information and social media age has been coming from U.S. companies, not Europeans...may be due to the fact that the hostile regulatory environment with broad prohibitions on data processing technologies [in Europe] has been deterring early-stage entrepreneurs and investors."[28]

Some also believe that tougher federal legislation is not the best approach to privacy issues. Thomas H. Davenport wrote recently in the *Wall Street Journal* that "[t]he downside to stronger laws is that the current Washington incumbents—particularly those in Congress—can't be trusted to do a good job of crafting privacy legislation."[29] Countering

---

[25] Russell R. Densmore, *Privacy Program Management: Tools for Managing Privacy Within Your Organization*, 49 (2013); see also Press Release, *DAA Self-Regulatory Program, DAA Announces Guidance for Self-Reg Principles in Mobile Environment*, available at http://www.aboutads.info/.

[26] Katy Bachman, *FTC's Olhausen Favors Privacy Self-Regulation: Commissioner's DAA keynote endears her to ad community*, ADWEEK.COM, Jun. 5, 2013, http://www.adweek.com/news/technology/ftcs-ohlhausen-favors-privacy-self-regulation-150036.

[27] Lothar Determann, *Social Media Privacy: A Dozen Myths and Facts*, 7 STAN. TECH. L. REV at 4 (2012).

[28] *Id.* at 6.

[29] *Should the U.S. Adopt European-Style Data-Privacy Protections*, WALL STREET J, Mar. 8, 2013, available at http://online.wsj.com/news/articles/SB1000142412788732433860457832 839379712709.

this view, Joel R. Reidenberg claimed in the same article that self-regulation has failed because "[i]ndustry self-regulation and options like privacy settings on social networks, Web browsers and mobile apps have failed to keep up with advances in invasive tracking techniques. Our limited legal rights don't come close to protecting us against online tracking and profiling."[30]

Viviane Reding, who is the vice president of the European Commission and the official responsible for basic rights, including data protection, typifies the EU approach that self-regulation needs to be backed up with enforcement. She has said that self-regulation "can be little more than a fig leaf" unless "there is strong, legally binding regulation in the first place."[31]

---

[30] *Id.*

[31] Cecilia Kang, *Q&A: EU Chief Privacy Regulator on New Internet Rules*, WASH. POST, Nov. 16, 2011, *available at* http://www.washingtonpost.com/blogs/post-tech/post/qanda-eu-chief-privacy-regulator-on-new-internet-rules/2011/11/15/gIQAOeZzRN_blog.htm.

2

US Federal Privacy and Data Protection Laws

The United States does not have a national baseline privacy law with an independent data protection authority. This country instead relies on laws for specific business sectors, such as medical or financial information, enforced by different arms of the federal government, as well as on self-governance and best practices. The Obama Administration has stopped short of calling for a single comprehensive federal law, but recommended in its 2012 Consumer Privacy Bill of Rights that legislation be adopted to "provide[] a baseline of clear protections for consumers and greater certainty for companies" to "supplement the existing framework and extend baseline protections to the sectors that existing Federal statutes do not cover."[1] In its March 2012 privacy report, the FTC similarly calls upon "Congress to consider enacting baseline privacy legislation and reiterates its call for data security legislation."[2]

Until gap-filling legislation such as that proposed by the White House and FTC is enacted, those navigating US privacy law must deal with a variety of federal laws applying to specific business sectors and types of conduct.

---

[1] The White House, *Consumer Data Privacy in a Networked World: A Framework for Protecting Privacy and Promoting Innovation in the Global Digital Economy* 1 (Feb. 2012) [hereinafter White House 2012 Report], http://www.whitehouse.gov/sites/default/files/privacy-final.pdf.

[2] Federal Trade Commission, *Protecting Consumer Privacy in an Era of Rapid Change: Recommendations for Businesses and Policymakers* i, viii., Mar. 2012, [hereinafter FTC 2012 Report], http://ftc.gov/os/2012/03/120326privacyreport.pdf. The FTC also called upon "industry to accelerate the pace of self-regulation."

The US Constitution

The closest the Constitution comes to implicitly referencing privacy is the Fourth Amendment, which protects the "right of the people to be secure in their persons, houses, papers, and effects, against unreasonable searches and seizures..." Interpreting this provision, the US Supreme Court has found that an "unreasonable" search or seizure is one that violates a person's "reasonable expectation of privacy."[3] In *Katz v. United States*, where the Supreme Court first expressed this view, a criminal defendant was found to have a "reasonable expectation of privacy" in the enclosed phone booth where he made calls placing illegal long-distance bets because he reasonably assumed that his conversation would "not be broadcast to the world."[4]

The Fourth Amendment applies only to the actions of governmental authorities and not to private parties. A person who believes that a business violated her reasonable expectations about the privacy of personal information therefore does not have a right to sue the business for violating her constitutional rights. Despite this restriction, the evolving nature of what is in fact a "reasonable expectation of privacy" under the Fourth Amendment affects privacy in non-constitutional contexts, particularly as privacy expectations are affected by technological change.

The 2012 case of *United States v. Jones* shows the overlap between the constitutional dimensions of privacy and changing public expectations. In *Jones*, the FBI placed a GPS tracking device on a narcotic suspect's car that gathered evidence that the suspect sought to keep out at trial under the Fourth Amendment. In holding that the search was unconstitutional, one Supreme Court Justice departed from the majority opinion to argue that there may be a reasonable expectation of privacy in information voluntarily disclosed to third parties. Assuming that there is *no* such expectation of privacy, said Justice Sotomayor, "is ill suited to the digital age, in which people reveal a great deal of information about themselves to third parties in the course of carrying out mundane tasks. People disclose the phone numbers that they dial or text to their cellular

---

[3] *Katz v. United States*, 389 U.S. 347, 351 (1967).
[4] *Id.* at 351-52.

providers; the URLs that they visit and the e-mail addresses with which they correspond to their Internet service providers; and the books, groceries, and medications they purchase to online retailers."[5]

The *Jones* case also shows that technology may produce unsettled privacy expectations. Justice Alito wrote in his concurring opinion that "[d]ramatic technological change may lead to periods in which popular expectations are in flux and may in the end produce significant changes in popular attitudes. New technology may provide increased convenience or security at the expense of privacy, and many people may find the tradeoff worthwhile. And even if the public does not welcome the diminution of privacy that new technology entails, they may eventually reconcile themselves to this development as inevitable."[6]

Despite the US Constitution's failure explicitly to mention privacy, the Supreme Court has also found privacy rights in other of its provisions. In *Griswold v. Connecticut*, Justice Douglas memorably found a right to privacy to use contraceptive devices in the "penumbras" of the "specific guarantees in the Bill of Rights...formed by emanations from those guarantees that help give them life and substance." These "[v]arious guarantees," Justice Douglas said, "create zones of privacy."[7] Because the right to data privacy involves private enterprises and not government actors, it is unlikely that Justice Douglas' "zones of privacy" will be extended to data privacy.

Federal Laws

The Privacy Act of 1974

The Privacy Act was an achievement of the first era of awareness about data privacy brought about by concerns about increased computerization of records. It was enacted on December 31, 1974 and signed into law by President Ford on January 1, 1975.[8] The Privacy Act, which was based to

---

[5] *United States v. Jones*, 132 S. Ct. 945, 957 (2012).
[6] *Id*. at 962.
[7] *Griswold v. Connecticut*, 381 U.S. 479, 484-85, 85 S.Ct. 1678, 1681 (1965).
[8] The Privacy Act, 5 U.S.C. § 552a (2010).

some extent on the FIPPs, establishes fair information practices for personal information systems maintained by the federal government.

The Privacy Act governs records maintained by federal agencies containing information about citizens or permanent residents. The law specifies that records may not be disclosed by government agencies to any person or another agency, "except pursuant to a written request by, or with the prior consent of, the individual to whom the record pertains..." Several exceptions exist to these restrictions, including "routine uses" within an agency and uses for archival purposes, civil or criminal law enforcement activities, documents provided to Congress, documents provided under court order, and documents provided to consumer reporting agencies.

The Privacy Act also allows people, upon request, to get access to documents about themselves and requires government agencies to provide public notice about the "systems of records" they maintain. The Privacy Act allows affected individuals to bring lawsuits for civil remedies when agencies do not comply with its provisions. If an agency has acted in a willful or intentional manner, an individual may be awarded actual damages but not less than $1,000, costs of action, and reasonable attorney fees, if the plaintiff can prove actual damages.[9]

Major exceptions to the Privacy Act are records maintained by the Central Intelligence Agency and agencies enforcing criminal laws. Heads of agencies may also promulgate rules exempting a system of records within the agency meeting specified conditions.

Despite its impressive name, the Privacy Act has been applied narrowly, partly because it deals only with records maintained by federal government agencies and because it includes many exceptions and exemptions. Some in Congress have called for modernization of the Privacy Act, because the definitions of "records" and "systems of records" under the Privacy Act have not kept up with advances in

---

[9] 5 U.S.C. § 552(a)(g)-(h). *See also Doe v. Chao*, 540 U.S. 614, 620, 124 S. Ct. 1204, 1208-09 (2004) (black lung claimants suing the Department of Labor for disclosing Social Security Numbers required to show actual harm to obtain damages).

technology.[10] Agencies have also made broad use of the "routine use" exception under the act to expand the number of the databases exempt from disclosure under the act.[11]

The Fair Credit Reporting Act of 1970 (FCRA)

The Fair Credit Reporting Act (FCRA) was enacted in 1970 to ensure that consumer reporting agencies exercise their responsibilities for the collection and dissemination of consumer credit information "with fairness, impartiality, and a respect for the consumer's right to privacy."[12] FCRA is one of the earliest federal consumer protection laws affecting privacy and is enforced by the FTC and private actions.

FCRA is a complex law that has been amended several times. Among FCRA's primary purposes is the regulation of "consumer reporting agencies"—entities that for a fee "regularly engage[] in whole or in part in the practice of assembling or evaluating consumer credit information or other information on consumers for the purpose of furnishing consumer reports to third parties."[13] FCRA regulates consumer reporting agencies as to "consumer reports," which are "written, oral or other communication of any information by a consumer reporting agency bearing on a consumer's credit worthiness, credit standing, credit capacity, character, general reputation, personal characteristics, or mode of living" used to establish the consumer's eligibility for credit, insurance, or employment.[14]

FCRA affects data privacy because it requires that data in consumer reports be confidential, accurate, relevant, and properly used. Consumers must receive notice if data is used to make adverse decisions, including denial of credit or employment. Consumers also have the right to know what information is contained about them in reports and can dispute inaccurate information with a consumer reporting agency. As discussed in Chapter 5,

---

[10] *See* Privacy Act Modernization for the Information Age Act of 2011, S. 1732, 112th Cong. (2011).
[11] *See* Electronic Privacy Information Center, *The Privacy Act of 1974*, http://epic.org/privacy/1974act/.
[12] The Fair Credit Reporting Act, 15 U.S.C. §§ 1681 *et seq.* (West).
[13] 15 U.S.C. § 1681(a)(f).
[14] 15 U.S.C. § 1681a(d).

consumer reporting agencies are not allowed to give information to employers or potential employers without the consumer's written consent. FCRA also specifies that consumer reporting agencies may only furnish consumer reports under specific stated circumstances.[15]

FCRA is enforced by the FTC and by a private right of action for plaintiffs who may obtain actual or statutory damages up to $1,000, punitive damages, and attorney's fees for willful violations. An example of private litigation under FCRA is a claim against a consumer reporting agency for negligent or willful failure to ensure the accuracy of information contained in the report where the agency was notified of an error and did not correct it. Class actions have also been filed against employers alleging that they improperly obtained consumer reports and took adverse employment actions without providing notice and a copy of the report to the person concerned.

The FTC has actively enforced FCRA and brought actions against entities operating as consumer reporting agencies that did not undertake appropriate consumer protection measures, including ensuring information sold is accurate and is being used for legally permissible purposes. In a recent case, a data broker paid $800,000 to settle charges that it marketed consumer profiles to the human resources, background screening and recruiting industries without taking the steps required by FCRA. In settling the case, the FTC announced that the broker violated the "three key requirements of the FCRA: to maintain reasonable procedures to verify who its users are and that the consumer report information would be used for a permissible purpose; to ensure accuracy of consumer reports; and to provide a user notice to any person that purchased its consumer reports."[16]

Entities that collect large amounts of information about consumers from a wide variety of sources for resale to customers—commonly referred to as "data brokers"—continue to be a major FTC focus. In its 2012 privacy

---

[15] The Federal Trade Commission, *A Summary of Your Rights Under the Fair Credit Reporting Act*, http://www.ftc.gov/os/2004/07/040709fcraappxf.pdf.
[16] Press Release, Federal Trade Commission, *Spokeo to Pay $800,000 to Settle FTC Charges Company Allegedly Marketed Information to Employers and Recruiters in Violation of FCRA* (June 12, 2012), http://www.ftc.gov/opa/2012/06/spokeo.shtm.

report, the FTC called for legislation to "address the invisibility of, and consumers' lack of control over, data brokers' collection and use of consumer information..." The proposed legislation would require data brokers to "(1) identify themselves to consumers and describe how they collect and use consumer data and (2) detail the access rights and other choices they provide with respect to the consumer data they maintain."[17] Because of the proliferation of data brokers offering personal information on the Internet, the FTC will likely continue to focus on these entities.

The Health Insurance Portability and Accountability Act of 1996 (HIPAA)

The Health Insurance Portability and Accountability Act of 1996 (HIPAA) establishes national standards for many aspects of health care, including coverage for people who change or lose their jobs. HIPAA also contains a "Privacy Rule" and a "Security Rule" that have a significant effect on protection of health information.

The HIPAA Privacy Rule[18]

The HIPAA Privacy Rule gives consumers rights to health care information, including rights to obtain copies of medical records, change incorrect information, and determine how information has been used and shared by doctors or insurers. The Privacy Rule requires "covered entities," which include health plans and insurance companies, health care providers, and health care clearinghouses, to follow procedures to protect the privacy of "protected health information." Employers, schools, law enforcement agencies, and workers' compensation carriers, among other entities, are generally not considered "covered entities."[19]

Protected health information includes all "individually identifiable health information" held or sent by a covered entity or by a business associate, in any form of media, whether electronic, paper or oral.[20] "Individually identifiable health information" is information and data related to a

---

[17] *See* FTC 2012 Report *supra* n. 1 at v, 68-70.
[18] HIPAA Privacy Rule, 45 C.F.R. §160, 45 C.F.R. §164 subparts A & E.
[19]Department of Health & Human Services, *Guidance Materials for Consumers, available at* http://www.hhs.gov/ocr/privacy/hipaa/understanding/consumers/index.html.
[20] *Id.*

person's "past, present or future physical or mental health or condition," "the provision of health care to the individual," or "the past, present, or future payment for the provision of health care to the individual" that "identifies the individual" or for which "there is a reasonable basis to believe it can be used to identify the individual."[21]

The Privacy Rule lists data "identifiers" that can be used to identify a person:

- Geographic subdivision smaller than a state;
- Birth date;
- Telephone or fax number;
- E-mail address;
- Social security number;
- Medical record number;
- Health plan beneficiary number;
- Account number;
- Certificate/license number;
- Vehicle identifier and serial number;
- Device identifier and serial number;
- URLs;
- IP addresses;
- Biometric identifiers;
- Full face photographic images; and
- "Any other unique identifying number, characteristic, or code."[22]

The Privacy Rule limits the circumstances in which protected health information can be disclosed by covered entities. Covered entities cannot disclose protected health information except as permitted by the Privacy Rule or authorized in writing. Permitted disclosures include:

- To the individual;
- For treatment, payment, and health care operations;
- In conjunction with an opportunity to agree or object;

---

[21] *Id.*

[22] 45 C.F.R. § 164.514 (listing elements of personal health information that if removed would render the information "de-identified").

- Incident to an otherwise permitted use and disclosure;
- For public interest and benefit activities; and
- As a limited data set for purpose of research, public health or health care operations.[23]

The Privacy Rule also requires covered entities to use, disclose, and ask for only the minimum necessary amount of protected health information. Covered entities must therefore have policies and procedures in place to restrict access by employees to protected health information based on employees' specific roles within an organization.

The HIPAA Security Rule[24]

The HIPAA Security Rule establishes national security standards for protecting health information held or transferred in electronic form. The Security Rule requires covered entities to put safeguards in place to secure electronic protected health information. Electronic protected health information is defined as individually identifiable information that is created, received, maintained or sent in electronic form.

The HIPAA Security Rule does not require specific security measures, but instead provides guidance to covered entities for adopting measures sufficient to ensure the confidentiality, integrity, and availability of electronic protected health information, protecting against reasonably anticipated threats and impermissible uses or disclosures, and ensuring compliance by their workforce. Covered entities must perform risk analysis as part of their security management processes and adopt administrative, physical, and technical safeguards.

The HITECH Act, which was enacted in 2009 to promote and expand health information technology, requires covered entities and their business associates to report data breaches of unsecured protected health information involving 500 or more people which "compromise[] the security or privacy of the protected health information." Notices of breaches must be made to the US Department of Health and Human

---

[23] 45 C.F.R. §164.502(a)(1).
[24] HIPAA Security Rule, 45 C.F.R. § 160 & 45 C.F.R. § 164 subparts A and C.

Services and prominent media outlets, as well as to those whose health information was breached.[25]

HIPAA Omnibus Rule

On September 23, 2013, the final regulations of the Department of Health and Human Services implementing the HITECH Act went into effect. These regulations, which are generally referred to as the "HIPAA Omnibus Rule," have been described by one government official as "the most sweeping changes to the HIPAA Privacy and Security Rules since they were first implemented."[26]

The HIPAA Omnibus Rule expands obligations for notifying patients regarding breaches of personal health information unless there is a "low probability of PHI compromise." The rule has changed from a subjective to a more objective standard and includes guidance for conducting a risk assessment relating to potential harm from a breach. The relevant factors for an assessment include the nature and extent of the information involved, the person who obtained unauthorized access, whether the information was actually acquired or accessed, and the extent to which the risk has been mitigated.[27]

The rule also affects privacy by preventing disclosure of information for services for which a patient has paid out-of-pocket to health plans, limiting the marketing and fund-raising communications that may be provided to patients without written authorization, prohibiting the sale of health information without authorization, and prohibiting sending unencrypted e-mails unless a patient has been advised of the risk and still requests that form of transmission.[28]

The Omnibus Rule also expands the range of individuals and entities that are treated as "business associates" under HIPAA. Under the rule, business

---

[25] 45 C.F.R. §§ 164.402 *et seq.*
[26] American Medical Association, *The Health Insurance Portability and Accountability Act (HIPAA) Omnibus Final Rule Summary,* http://www.ama-assn.org/resources/doc/ washington/hipaa-omnibus-final-rule-summary.pdf.
[27] *Id.*
[28] *Id.*

associates are responsible for their subcontractors and have to abide by the HIPAA Privacy and Security Rules. The rule also increases penalties under HIPAA to a maximum of $1.5 million for a violation.[29]

HIPAA Enforcement

The Office for Civil Rights of the Department of Health and Human Services (OCR) enforces the Privacy and Security Rules and conducts investigations and compliance reviews. There is no private right of action for violation of these rules. The Office for Civil Rights may impose penalties on covered entities depending upon whether the covered entity engaged in willful neglect.

The Office for Civil Rights has enforced the Privacy and Security Rules in a variety of situations, including unauthorized disclosure by a hospital to an employer, impermissible disclosure of protected health information in response to a subpoena, improper access by a covered entity's employees of medical records, failure to follow privacy requirements in leaving telephone messages, and not providing notice of privacy practices.

In one of the more prominent recent cases, a managed care company paid $1.7 million for failing to put in place appropriate administrative and technical safeguards, including failing to verify the identity of those seeking access to electronic protected health information and impermissibly disclosing on the Internet the health information of over 600,000 people.[30] In another case, a medical provider was fined $1.5 million because of a data breach due to the theft of an unencrypted personal laptop containing the electronic health information of patients and research subjects.[31]

In a widely reported case, a university-run health system settled violations of the Privacy and Security Rules when employees accessed the medical

---

[29] *Id.*
[30] Press Release, Department of Health & Human Services, *WellPoint Pays HHS $1.7 million for leaving information accessible over internet*, (Jul. 11, 2013), http://www.hhs.gov/news/press/2013pres/07/20130711b.html.
[31] Department of Health & Human Services, *Massachusetts Provider Settles HIPAA Case for $1.5 million*, http://www.hhs.gov/ocr/privacy/hipaa/enforcement/examples/meei-agreement.html.

records of celebrity patients.[32] A managed care plan also had to pay $1.2 million after CBS Evening News reported that it had bought a photocopier previously leased by the plan that contained confidential medical data on its hard drive.[33] Given the sensitivity of protected health information, it is likely that the Office for Civil Rights will continue actively to enforce the HIPAA Privacy and Security Rules.

The Gramm-Leach-Bliley Act of 1999 (GLB)

The Gramm-Leach-Bliley Act (GLB), also known as the Financial Services Modernization Act, is a financial services modernization measure enacted in 1999.[34] The primary purpose of GLB was to remove barriers in the financial services industry among banks, security firms, and insurance companies. Because of several prominent reports of data misuse, including a bank that sold millions of credit card numbers to adult website companies, GLB also contains financial privacy and safeguards rules imposing obligations on financial institutions for sharing and protecting "nonpublic financial information."

GLB Financial Privacy Rule

GLB requires "financial institutions" to provide privacy notices to consumers and customers explaining their information sharing practices. GLB also gives customers the right to limit sharing of *some* of their "nonpublic personal information."

"Financial institution" is broadly defined under GLB as a business that significantly engages in financial activities, including lending or safeguarding money or securities, insuring or indemnifying against loss, harm, damage, illness, disability or death, providing financial investment or economic advisory services or underwriting or dealing with securities. Financial institutions include:

---

[32] Department of Health & Human Services, *UCLA Health System Settle Potential Violation of the HIPAA Privacy and Security Rules*, http://www.hhs.gov/ocr/privacy/hipaa/enforcement/examples/uclaagreement.html.

[33] iHealthBeat, *Affinity Health Plan to Pay HHS $1.2M over Patient Data Breach* (Aug. 15, 2013), http://www.ihealthbeat.org/articles/2013/8/15/affinity-health-plan-to-pay-hhs-12m-over-patient-data-breach.

[34] 15 U.S.C. § 6801 *et seq.* (West).

- Banks;
- Mortgage lenders and brokers;
- Check cashers;
- Pay-day lenders;
- Credit counseling services;
- Financial or investment advisory services;
- Retailers that issue their own credit cards;
- Auto dealers that lease and/or finance;
- Collection agency services;
- Sellers of money orders and traveler's checks; and
- Government entities providing financial products such as student loans or mortgages.[35]

Examples of entities that are *not* subject to GLB include retailers that do not issue their own credit cards, grocery stores allowing consumers to get cash back, and merchants allowing people to "run a tab."[36]

"Consumers," as defined by GLB, are persons obtaining financial products from financial institutions used primarily for personal, family, or household purposes. Consumers do not include commercial clients, such as business entities. "Customers" is a defined subclass of consumers with a continuing relationship with a financial institution, including individuals opening a credit card account or getting a loan.[37]

Nonpublic personal information includes nonpublic personally identifiable financial information used to obtain a financial product or service and information about a consumer resulting from a transaction involving a financial product or services. Nonpublic personal information includes the fact that a person is a customer of a bank, name, address, social security number and account number, information provided in a loan application, and information on consumer reports.

---

[35] Federal Trade Commission Bureau of Consumer Protection Division of Financial Practices, *The Gramm-Leach-Bliley Act Privacy of Consumer Financial Information,* http://www.ftc.gov/privacy/glbact/glboutline.htm.
[36] *Id.*
[37] *Id.*

In contrast, "publicly available information" is information that a financial institution has a "reasonable basis to believe" is lawfully made available to the general public from government records, widely distributed media, and legally required disclosures. Such information includes numbers listed in telephone books, information posted on a website, and information in public real estate records.[38]

GLB mandates that a financial institution give customers "clear and conspicuous" notice of its information sharing practices when a person becomes a customer and then on an annual basis. These notices must include, among other things, the categories of nonpublic personal information that an institution collects and discloses, as well as the affiliates and non-affiliated third parties to whom it discloses the information. The notice must also describe the financial institution's policies and practices for protecting the confidentiality and security of nonpublic personal information. The notice must explain the customer's right to opt out, as well as a "reasonable means" for opting out of some disclosures.

Customers are allowed to opt out of having their nonpublic personal information shared by financial institutions with *non-affiliated* companies, but not with *affiliated* companies. The burden is on the customer to exercise this right. Moreover, financial institutions are allowed to share nonpublic personal information with third parties for processing transactions and for some marketing purposes.[39]

GLB Safeguards Rule

The GLB Safeguards Rule mandates that financial institutions secure and maintain the confidentiality of nonpublic personal information. The rule requires companies to develop written information security plans describing the ways in which they protect information. Among the requirements for such plans are:

- Designation of one or more employees to coordinate information security programs;

---

[38] *Id.*
[39] *Id.*

- Identification and assessment of risks to customer information and effectiveness of current safeguards;
- Design and implementation (and later monitoring) of a safeguards program;
- Selection of vendors and service providers that can maintain appropriate safeguards; and
- Evaluation and adjustment of the program.[40]

Although the FTC has said that the Safeguards Rule is designed to give companies implementation flexibility, it has also recommended that companies:

- Perform background checks on employees;
- Limit access to customer records on a need-to-know basis;
- Control access to sensitive information;
- Develop proper technology policies;
- Secure physical records;
- Impose disciplinary measures for violations of the policy;
- Perform assessments about the location and security of customer information;
- Take steps to ensure the secure transmission of customers' information;
- Securely dispose of information;
- Monitor security threats;
- Maintain up-to-date security procedures and software patches;
- Put in place appropriate audit procedures; and
- Deal with and notify customers about security breaches.[41]

GLB also encourages financial institutions to adopt safeguards against pretexting, which is obtaining nonpublic information without proper authority. Pretexting includes using false representations, fictitious documents, and forgery.[42]

---

[40] Federal Trade Commission, *Financial Institutions and Customer Information: Complying with the Safeguards Rule*, Apr. 2006, http://business.ftc.gov/documents/bus54-financial-institutions-and-customer-information-complying-safeguards-rule.

[41] *Id.*

[42] Press Release, Federal Trade Commission, *FTC Kicks off "Operation Detect Pretext"* (Jan. 31, 2001), *available at* http://www.ftc.gov/opa/2001/01/pretexting.shtm.

GLB Enforcement

GLB is enforced by the FTC, financial industry regulators, and state attorney generals. It does not confer a private right of action. Using its enforcement authority, the FTC has required mortgage companies that failed to protect customers' information to have their information security programs certified by an independent professional and to conduct biannual audits of the programs.[43] The FTC has also brought charges against credit report resellers for not taking reasonable information security steps to protect consumers' data, including allowing hackers to access more than 1,800 credit reports.[44]

In another case, the FTC brought a complaint under the pretexting provision of GLB against a mortgage spamming operation using deception to trick consumers into sharing personal financial data. The company set up a website pretending to be a mortgage lender requiring consumers to input sensitive personal information that the company then sold to nonaffiliated third parties without consumers' consent.[45]

The Children's Online Privacy Protection Act of 1998 (COPPA)

The Children's Online Privacy Protection Act (COPPA)[46] was enacted in 1998 and became effective in 2000. COPPA regulates the online collection of information from children less than thirteen years of age. The FTC, which enforces COPPA, has promulgated regulations referred to as the "COPPA Rule." The most recent version of the COPPA Rule became effective July 1, 2013.

The FTC has said that "[t]he primary goal of COPPA is to place parents in control over what information is collected from their young children

---

[43] Press Release, Federal Trade Commission, *FTC Enforces Gramm-Leach-Bliley Act's Safeguards Rule Against Mortgage Companies* (Nov. 16, 2004), *available at* http://www.ftc.gov/opa/2004/11/ns.shtm.

[44] Press Release, Federal Trade Commission, *FTC Approves Final Orders Settling Charges that Credit Report Resellers Allowed Hackers to Access Consumers' Personal Information* (Aug. 19, 2011), *available at* http://ftc.gov/opa/2011/08/creditreporters.shtm.

[45] Press Release, Federal Trade Commission, *Deceptive Mortgage Scam Halted* (Mar. 20, 2003), *available at* http://www.ftc.gov/opa/2003/03/thirty6.shtm.

[46] 15 U.S.C. §§ 6601-6506 (West).

online."[47] COPPA applies to the operators of websites and mobile apps that are "directed" to children under thirteen collecting personal information from children, as well as operators of "general audience websites or online services with actual knowledge that they are collecting, using, or disclosing personal information from children under 13."[48] Operators of such websites must:

- Post a clear and prominently labeled online privacy policy identifying the names of operators collecting or maintaining information and their practices for personal information obtained from children;
- Give notice to parents to obtain verifiable parental consent before collecting personal information from children;
- Allow parents the choice of consenting to the operator's collection of personal information, but prohibiting the disclosure of that information to third parties;
- Give parents access to a child's personal information for review or deletion;
- Give parents the right to prevent further use or online collection of a child's personal information;
- Maintain the confidentiality, security, and integrity of the information; and
- Retain personal information collected online only as long as it is necessary to fulfill the purpose for which it was collected and delete the information using reasonable measures to protect against its unauthorized access or use.[49]

Under the revised COPPA Rule, parental notifications should function as an "effective 'just-in-time' message about an operator's information practices, while also directing parents online to view any additional information contained in the operator's online notice."[50]

---

[47] Bureau of Consumer Protection, *Complying with COPPA*, (rev. Jul. 2013), *available at* http://business.ftc.gov/documents/Complying-with-COPPA-Frequently-Asked-Questions.
[48] *Id.*
[49] *Id.*
[50] *Id.*

The application of the COPPA Rule to any specific situation may be complex, given ongoing technological changes and the considerable variety of websites collecting and distributing personal information. Under the revised COPPA Rule, personal information encompasses not only names, addresses, telephone, and social security numbers, but "persistent identifiers" used to identify users over time and across different websites. In addition, personal information includes geolocation information sufficient to identify the street name and location of a person, photos or videos, and screen or user names.[51]

The revised COPPA Rule also expands the range of applicable websites to include sites that integrate outside services collecting personal information from visitors, including plug-ins or advertising networks. Moreover, "online services" include those that connect to the Internet or to wide-area networks, such as mobile networks and Internet-enabled location based services.[52]

One of the greater challenges presented by COPPA is whether a website is "directed to children." Under the revised COPPA Rule, operators of websites must consider a number of factors in making this determination, including the subject matter of the website, its visual content, use of animated characters, music or other audio content, the age of the models depicted, presence of child celebrities, language, and whether the advertising present on the website is directed to children.[53]

If a website is directed to children, the operator cannot age screen and block users who identify as being under the age of thirteen. However, if a website has children as a secondary audience, it may use age screens to differentiate between child and non-child users and offer different activities to such users.[54]

COPPA does not apply to all information involving children on the Internet. It pertains only to information *from* children, not information *about* children.

---

[51] *Id.*
[52] *Id.*
[53] *Id.*
[54] *Id.*

COPPA does not prevent parents or other adults from posting information about children on the Internet. Children may also take part in interactive communities without parental consent if the communities take care to delete children's personal information before it goes public.[55]

COPPA contains no private right of action but is instead enforced by the FTC. The FTC has enforced COPPA in a number of contexts. In 2012, the FTC required an operator of fan websites for music stars such as Justin Bieber and Rihanna to pay $1 million to settle charges that it had collected children's personal information without parental consent. The operator violated COPPA by obtaining children's personal information to allow them to subscribe to fan newsletters and create profiles, despite claiming that it did not collect information without prior parental consent.[56] Similarly, the FTC fined a business operating a website that allowed children to register, create, and update profile information, create public posts, and upload pictures and videos, for registering children without collecting parents' e-mail addresses or obtaining permission for their children to take part in the site.[57] The FTC has fined a company $800,000 for collecting personal information from consumers and children from their mobile device address books without their knowledge or consent.[58]

Electronic Communications Privacy Act (ECPA) and the Stored Communications Act (SCA) of 1986

The Electronic Communications Privacy Act (ECPA) of 1986[59] extends wiretapping protections to transmissions of electronic data, including by cell phone and the Internet. ECPA prohibits intentional interceptions of electronic communications using electronic devices. It was enacted to

---

[55] *Id.*

[56] Press Release, Federal Trade Commission, *Operator of Celebrity Fan Websites to Pay $1 million to Settle FTC Charges that It Illegally Collected Children's Information Without Their Parents' Consent* (Oct. 4, 2012), *available at* http://www.ftc.gov/opa/2012/10/artistarena.shtm.

[57] Press Release, Federal Trade Commission, *Operator of Social Networking Website for Kids Settles FTC Charges Site Collected Kids' Personal Information Without Parental Consent* (Nov. 8, 2011), *available at* http://www.ftc.gov/opa/2011/11/skidekids.shtm.

[58] Federal Trade Commission, *Path Social Networking App Settles FTC Charges It Deceived Consumers and Improperly Collected Personal Information from Users' Mobile Address Books* (Feb. 1, 2013), *available at* http://www.ftc.gov/opa/2013/02/path.shtm.

[59] 18 U.S.C. §§ 2510 *et seq.* (West).

create "a fair balance between the privacy expectations of citizens and the legitimate needs of law enforcement."[60]

ECPA contains the Wiretap Act, which addresses the interception of communications, the Stored Communications Act (SCA), which governs communications at rest, and the Pen-Register Act, which applies to access to the non-content information about a call, such as the origin and destination of a communication. Violators of the ECPA may be jailed or fined. Those whose rights have been violated may also bring civil lawsuits for actual damages, besides obtaining punitive damages and attorney fees.

Courts have struggled to interpret the Wiretap Act in the context of modern technological developments, given that the law predates the widespread adoption of the Internet and some current forms of electronic communication. However, the Wiretap Act generally prohibits intercepting communications and disclosing communications known to violate the act. A communication must also be private for there to be a violation of the Wiretap Act.

The Stored Communications Act (SCA), which is part of ECPA, prohibits unauthorized access to communications at rest, primarily e-mails not in transit. Although the government requires a warrant to obtain access to e-mail in transit, in storage on a home computer, and unopened e-mails in remote storage, it only requires a subpoena for opened e-mails in remote storage or unopened e-mails stored for more than 180 days.[61] This aspect of the law has been criticized for failing to keep up with technological change and for the large number of requests made by government agencies to companies such as Google, Verizon and Facebook. Indeed, some Internet companies and consumer advocates claim that "letters in a file cabinet" now have more protection than "e-mail on a server."[62]

---

[60] Electronic Privacy Information Center, *Electronic Communications Privacy Act (ECPA)*, http://epic.org/privacy/ecpa/.
[61] *Id.*
[62] Miguel Helft & Claire Cain Miller, *1986 Privacy Law is Outrun by the Web*, N.Y. TIMES, Jan. 9, 2011, *available at* http://www.nytimes.com/2011/01/10/technology/10privacy.html? pagewanted=all&_r=0.

Although the Wiretap Act and SCA are criminal statutes, private parties are able to bring lawsuits under these statutes. For the Wiretap Act, the plaintiff must show that there has been an intentional interception of an electronic communication.[63] Under the SCA, a plaintiff must show that there was intentional access without authorization to "a facility through which an electronic communication service is provided" and access to "a wire or electronic communication while it is in electronic storage in such system."[64] The intersection and application of the two laws often presents difficult problems.[65] Examples of privacy litigation brought under the ECPA and the SCA are discussed in Chapter 8.

The Computer Fraud and Abuse Act of 1986 (CFAA)

The Computer Fraud and Abuse Act of 1986 (CFAA)[66] makes it a crime to intentionally access a computer "without authorization" or to "exceed authorized access." The CFAA encompasses seven offenses:

- Obtaining national security information;
- Compromising confidentiality;
- Trespassing in a government computer;
- Accessing computers to defraud and obtain value;
- Damaging a computer or information;
- Trafficking in passwords; and
- Threatening to damage a computer.[67]

A plaintiff may bring a civil lawsuit under the CFAA, even though it is a criminal law, if the plaintiff can show damage caused by a violation of one of the law's substantive provisions and conduct prohibited by the act.

The US government has used the CFAA to prosecute persons or entities in several contexts, including actions undertaken by business competitors

---

[63] 18 U.S.C. § 2511(1)(a).
[64] 18 U.S.C. § 2701(a)(1).
[65] *See, e.g., Konop v. Hawaiian Airlines, Inc.,* 302 F.3d 868, 874 (9th Cir. 2002) (observing that the intersection of the Wiretap Act and SCA "is a complex, often convoluted area of the law").
[66] 18 U.S.C. § 1030 (2008).
[67] Electronic Frontier Foundation, *Computer Fraud and Abuse Act (CFAA)*, https://ilt.eff.org/index.php/Computer_Fraud_and_Abuse_Act_(CFAA).

against one another, hacking, and acts directed at computers. Although some argue the law was enacted primarily with hackers in mind, the government has also prosecuted those who have violated corporate policies, including employees exceeding their authorized access to computers.

In a recent case, the Ninth Circuit Court of Appeals rejected this use of the CFAA, holding that a former employee of an executive search firm did not violate the law by exceeding his employer's restrictions on computer use. The court refused to criminalize those activities because it said that would mean that "millions of unsuspecting individuals would find that they are engaging in criminal conduct" by activities such as "g-chatting with friends, playing games, shopping or watching sports highlights."[68]

The CFAA has engendered controversy, particularly after the death of Aaron Swartz, who was charged with violating the CFAA by downloading a large number of scholarly articles from MIT.[69] Proposals for amending the law have been mooted, including redefining the term "exceeds authorized access" to remove some of the current law's ambiguities and requiring that the conduct be akin to hacking, not violation of use policies.

Examples of privacy litigation brought under the CFAA are discussed in Chapter 8.

Other Federal Privacy Laws

Many other federal laws have privacy implications for certain types of communications or information. These laws include:

- Telephone Consumer Protection Act of 1991 (TCPA)[70] restricting unsolicited telemarketing calls to homes, including establishing allowable times for such calls and requiring callers to provide information to consumers.

---

[68] *United States v. Nosal*, 676 F.3d 854, 860 (9th Cir. 2012).
[69] Electronic Frontier Foundation, *Computer Fraud and Abuse Act Reform*, https://www.eff. org/issues/cfaa.
[70] 47 U.S.C. § 227 (2010).

- Driver's Privacy Protection Act of 1994 (DPPA)[71] prohibiting disclosure of personal information by state Departments of Motor Vehicles without permission of the person to whom the information applies, with exceptions for permissible uses.

- Video Privacy Protection Act of 1988 (VPPA)[72] prohibiting wrongful disclosure of personally identifiable information concerning consumers by "videotape service providers," including rental records, without the consumer's consent.

- Telemarketing Sales Rule (TSR) (A Rule Promulgated by the FTC)[73] allowing consumers to restrict the telemarketing calls received at home. TSR establishes the National Do Not Call Registry by which consumers can register their telephone numbers to prevent telemarketing calls.

- Controlling the Assault of Non-Solicited Pornography and Marketing Act of 2003 (CAN-SPAM)[74] establishing rules for commercial messages (not just bulk e-mails), including messages to consumers and businesses. CAN-SPAM prohibits false or misleading headers and deceptive subject lines, and requires messages be identified as ads. The act also requires senders to identify where they are located and to tell recipients how to opt out of receiving future messages. CAN-SPAM includes messages sent to wireless phones and pagers if they contain an Internet domain name.

- The Red Flags Rule (A Regulation Issued Under the Fair and Accurate Credit Transaction Act of 2003)[75] requiring businesses and other organizations to put in place a written identity theft prevention program designed to identify and detect relevant "red flags" of such theft, prevent and mitigate identify theft, and periodically update identity theft programs as technology changes. The Red Flags Rule specifies some categories of "common red flags," including alerts from credit reporting agencies, suspicious documents, inconsistent personal information, and suspect account activity.

---

[71] 18 U.S.C. §§ 2721 *et seq.* (2000).
[72] 18 U.S.C. § 2710 (2013).
[73] 16 C.F.R. §§ 310 *et seq.* (2010).
[74] 15 U.S.C. §§ 7701 *et seq.* (2004).
[75] 17 C.F.R. §§ 162 *et seq.* (2011).

3

US State Privacy Laws

Individual states in the United States have enacted a wide range of laws affecting the privacy of personal data. Under the federal system, states are generally allowed to adopt laws on matters affecting commerce within their own borders without preemption by the federal government. States have taken advantage of the lack of a comprehensive federal privacy and data protection regime to act in areas where the federal government has not legislated or to add to the protections given by federal laws.

The resulting complex of inconsistent state privacy laws can be a source of confusion to enterprises operating in multiple jurisdictions. The 2012 White House report on privacy said that the plethora of state security breach notification laws "creates significant burdens for companies without much countervailing benefit for consumers."[1] Until Congress passes more comprehensive privacy and data security laws, businesses and consumers must continue to deal with the complex of state privacy and data security laws.

This summary concentrates on California with occasional references to other state laws.[2] Several reasons exist for highlighting California law. California undoubtedly has been the most active state in enacting laws addressing privacy of personal data. In some areas, such as the data breach notification

---

[1] The White House, *Consumer Data Privacy in a Networked World: A Framework for Protecting Privacy and Promoting Innovation in the Global Digital Economy* 39 (Feb. 2012) [hereinafter White House 2012 Report], http://www.whitehouse.gov/sites/default/files/privacy-final.pdf.

[2] A useful compendium of California and federal privacy laws may be found on the California Attorney General's website http://oag.ca.gov/privacy/privacy-laws.

laws discussed below in Chapter 6, California was the first in the field, and its example has inspired other states to enact similar laws. In other fields, such as the state's "Shine the Light Law," California's example has not yet been followed by other states, but nonetheless addresses an important aspect of data privacy affecting many businesses. Moreover, because many of the major technology and Internet companies are based in California, its laws have greater impact than those of other states and often establish a *de facto* national standard.

State Constitutions

Several states, including Alaska, California, Florida, Hawaii, and Montana, have explicit constitutional rights to privacy. Article 1, Section 1 of the California Constitution states, "All people are by nature free and independent and have inalienable rights. Among these are enjoying and defending life and liberty, acquiring, possessing, and protecting property, and pursuing and obtaining safety, happiness, and privacy."

Article II, Section 10 of the Montana Constitution provides that "[t]he right of individual privacy is essential to the well-being of a free society and shall not be infringed without a showing of a compelling state interest." Notably, the California and Montana constitutional privacy provisions date to 1972 when there were concerns about "'government snooping,' computer stored and generated 'dossiers' and 'cradle-to-grave' profiles on every American."[3]

The California constitutional right to privacy allows private actions not only against the government but against non-government entities. In a leading case, the California Supreme Court concluded that an invasion of privacy under the California Constitution requires "(1) a legally protected privacy interest; (2) a reasonable expectation of privacy in the circumstances; and (3) conduct by defendant constituting a serious invasion of privacy." The court ruled that the right to privacy is not absolute and that a defendant may prove "that the invasion of privacy is justified because it substantively furthers one or more countervailing interests."[4]

---

[3] *Hill v. Nat'l Collegiate Athletic Assn.*, 7 Cal. 4th 1, 21 (1994) (quoting the ballot argument for the initiative that led to the inclusion of privacy in Article I of the California Constitution).
[4] *Id.* at 39-40.

Plaintiffs claiming a violation of privacy rights involving personal data in California face challenges in showing that they have suffered a "serious invasion of privacy." A plaintiff complaining that the constitutional right to privacy was violated by a retailer collecting ZIP codes under "false pretenses and using [them] for its own marketing purposes" was found not to have suffered a "serious" invasion of privacy because the plaintiff had not shown an "egregious breach of social norms, but routine commercial behavior."[5] In cases involving security breaches of personal information, courts have also concluded that a mere "risk of privacy invasion, rather than an actual privacy invasion," is not a violation of the constitutional right to privacy.[6]

In states where there is no explicit constitutional right to privacy, courts have recognized some privacy rights, including rights to personal autonomy for procreation, parental and reproductive rights, marriage and intimate associations.[7] Other states, including New York, have state constitutional provisions similar to the US Constitution's Fourth Amendment or provide, as do the Constitutions of Arizona and Washington, that "[n]o person shall be disturbed in his private affairs, or his home invaded, without authority of law."[8] Despite these provisions, state constitutional privacy rights have not often been extended to personal data.

Privacy of Medical Information

The data breach notification laws of many states, including California, Delaware, Missouri, North Dakota, Texas and others, require notification of breaches of medical or health insurance information. In addition, most states protect the confidentiality of medical information.

California's Confidentiality of Medical Information Act (CMIA) requires providers or contractors of health care to maintain the privacy of medical

---

[5] *Fogelstrom v. Lamps Plus, Inc.*, 195 Cal. App. 4th 986, 992 (2011) (quoting *Hill*, 7 Cal. 4th at 37).

[6] *Ruiz v. Gap, Inc.*, 380 F.App'x. 689, 693 (9th Cir. 2010).

[7] Jeffrey M. Shaman, *The Right of Privacy in State Constitutional Law*, 37 RUTGERS LAW J. 971 (2006).

[8] AZ CONST. art II, § 8; WA CONST. art I, § 7.

information.[9] CMIA prohibits disclosure of medical information without first obtaining authorization with exceptions for court orders, search warrants, and coroners.[10] "Medical information" is defined broadly as "any individually identifiable information, in electronic or physical form, in possession of or derived from a provider of health care, health care service plan, pharmaceutical company, or contractor regarding a patient's medical history, mental or physical condition, or treatment."[11]

CMIA obligates providers of health care, health care service plans, pharmaceutical companies, and contractors to preserve the confidentiality of medical information.[12] An entity that "negligently creates, maintains, preserves, stores, abandons, destroys, or disposes of medical information" is subject to remedies and penalties, including damages, administrative fines, and civil penalties. Civil lawsuits are allowed "against any person or entity who has negligently released confidential information or records concerning him or her," including $1,000 in "nominal damages." To obtain such damages it is not necessary that the plaintiff "suffered or was threatened with actual damages."[13]

Plaintiffs have taken advantage of the $1,000 "nominal damages" provision in the CMIA and filed class actions when medical information was lost in a breach. For example, when a burglar stole a computer from a health care facility containing unencrypted medical and identifying information for an estimated 4.24 million patients, the facility was sued for billions of dollars in several class actions.[14]

Privacy of Consumer Information

Although surveys find that many consumers are concerned about the ways in which their personal information is used for marketing purposes,

---

[9] Ann. Cal. Civ. Code § 56 *et seq.* (West).
[10] Ann. Cal. Civ. Code § 56.10(a)-(b) (West).
[11] Ann. Cal. Civ. Code § 56.05(g) (West).
[12] Ann. Cal. Civ. Code § 56.101 (West).
[13] Ann. Cal. Civ. Code §§ 56.101, 56.36 (West).
[14] California Healthline, *11 Class-Action Suits Combined as Single Case over Sutter Data Breach*, Mar. 2, 2012, http://www.californiahealthline.org/articles/2012/3/2/11-class-action-lawsuits-over-sutter-data-breach-grouped-in-sacramento.

few federal and state laws address the subject. Aside from the FTC's enforcement efforts requiring businesses to follow their privacy policies and its enforcement of various federal laws, only California has a law relating to the use of personal information by businesses.

California's "Shine the Light" law[15] is directed to the business practice of compiling and selling individuals' personal information for direct marketing purposes. Under the law, for profit companies doing business in California must either allow California residents with whom they have an established business relationship to opt out of having their information shared or disclose the ways in which personal information was used by third parties for direct marketing purposes within the last calendar year.[16] The disclosures are not specific to a person, but instead include the categories of personal information that the company disclosed and the third parties that received the information.[17] Among the categories of personal information that a business must disclose are e-mail addresses, names of children, religion, occupation, education, political party affiliation, social security and bank account numbers, education, and payment history.[18]

If a business fails to comply with the law by submitting incomplete information or by not responding to a disclosure request, the business has a ninety-day grace period to provide complete information. If requests are not responded to after ninety days, a customer may institute a lawsuit for civil damages. Violations are also punishable with a civil penalty of no more than $500 or for willful violations of no more than $3000.

Privacy of Credit and Credit Cards

Many states have enacted laws supplementing FCRA for credit reporting agencies and consumer reports. States have specified the length of time that information such as arrest or bankruptcy records may be included on a credit report. Other states have laws addressing the rights of consumers to obtain credit reports, regulating consumer reporting agencies, or restricting the information that may be placed on credit cards slips.

---

[15] Ann. Cal. Civ. Code § 1798.83 (West).
[16] *Id.*
[17] Ann. Cal. Civ. Code § 1798.84 (West).
[18] Ann. Cal. Civ. Code § 1798.83(6)(A) (West).

An example of one such a law is California's Song-Beverly Credit Card Act (Song-Beverly) enacted in 1971.[19] Song-Beverly prohibits businesses from asking for or requiring personal identification information on credit card transaction forms. Under the law, personal identification information is defined as "information concerning the cardholder, other than information set forth on the credit card, and including, but not limited to, the cardholder's address and telephone number."[20] In a 2011 decision, the California Supreme Court concluded that a credit cardholder's ZIP code is personal identification information.[21]

Because plaintiffs are entitled to bring private lawsuits and obtain civil penalties of up to $1,000 per transaction, plus costs and legal fees, many lawsuits have been brought challenging the practice of obtaining ZIP codes for transactions. To cite one instance, customers purchasing apps from Apple's iTunes service brought a lawsuit alleging that Apple violated Song-Beverly by collecting their personal information online. The California Supreme Court held that Song-Beverly did not apply to online transactions involving electronically downloadable products because online retailers need to protect against credit card fraud.[22] Because the court limited its holding to downloadable products, it is uncertain whether Song-Beverly applies to other types of Internet transactions, including purchases of physical items.

Privacy of Social Security Numbers

Most states have laws protecting social security numbers (SSNs) from display or restricting their collection.[23] California, for example, restricts use of SSNs by prohibiting:

---

[19] Ann. Cal. Civ. Code §§ 1747 *et seq.* (West).

[20] Ann. Cal. Civ. Code § 1747.08(b) (West).

[21] *Pineda v. Williams-Sonoma Stores, Inc.*, 51 Cal. 4th 524, 532-33 (2011). The Supreme Judicial Court of Massachusetts reached the same conclusion in *Tyler v. Michaels Stores, Inc.*, 464 Mass. 492 (2013), under that state's General Law Chapter 93 section 105 which governs obtaining personal information in conjunction with credit card transactions.

[22] *Apple v. Superior Court*, 56 Cal.4th 128 (2013).

[23] The Consumer's Union lists 19 states that restrict printing SSNs on ID cards, 22 states that restrict intentionally communicating SSNs to the public or public posting and display, and 17 that restrict mailing of SSNs within a mailing envelope. *See* Consumers Union, *State Laws Restricting Private Use of Social Security Numbers*, Jun. 2008, http://consumersunion.org/

- Public posting or display of a person's SSN;
- Printing the number on identification cards;
- Sending a SSN across the Internet unless the connection is secure or encrypted;
- Printing SSNs on mailings or forms or applications unless required by law;
- Encoding or embedding SSNs in a card or document using a bar code, chip, magnetic strip or other technology; and
- Printing more than the last four digits of an employee's SSN on pay stubs or itemized statements.[24]

California, like other states, does permit SSNs to be used if the use is required by state or federal law or for internal verification or administrative purposes. California law also requires reduction of collection and access to SSNs and protection of SSNs with security safeguards. For example, a California law requires businesses that own or license personal information about California residents to "implement and maintain reasonable security procedures and practices appropriate to the nature of the information, to protect the personal information from unauthorized access, destruction, use, modification or disclosure."[25]

Invasion of Privacy and Call Monitoring

Another frequent area for state legislation is regulation of electronic surveillance and call monitoring. Many state laws make it a criminal offense to intercept telephone calls without a party's consent or a court order. Although some laws allow recording of conversations if one party consents to the recording, other states, including California, Connecticut, Florida, Hawaii, Illinois, Maryland, Massachusetts, Montana, Nevada, New Hampshire, Pennsylvania, and Washington, require consent of *both* parties to the conversation.[26]

---

news/state-laws-restricting-private-use-of-social-security-numbers/.

[24] Cal. Civil Code § 1798.85 (West).

[25] Cal. Civil Code § 1798.81.5(b) (West), (The law does not apply to providers of health care, financial institutions, or "covered entities" under HIPAA).

[26] Digital Media Law Project, *Recording Phone Calls and Conversations*, Aug. 15, 2012, http://www.dmlp.org/legal-guide/recording-phone-calls-and-conversations.

California's Invasion of Privacy Act (CIPA) is a typical "two party" law requiring the consent of all parties to the conversation for recording of "confidential communications" where there is a "reasonable expectation of privacy."[27] In addition to criminal penalties, violations of the CIPA may lead to civil actions with a penalty of $5,000 per violation.[28]

For some years, the CIPA was most typically invoked in non-commercial situations. A particularly lurid example involved a manicurist who recorded a client's calls in which the client claimed she was injecting her husband with water instead of medicine for his prostate cancer. After the husband's death, the customer sued her manicurist and stepson for invasion of privacy under the CIPA. The California Supreme Court affirmed the jury's finding that the conversations were confidential because one of the parties reasonably expected that no one was overhearing the conversations.[29]

The California Court of Appeal in 2011 ruled that the CIPA applies where a corporate employee secretly monitored a conversation between a customer and another corporate employee for quality control purposes. Although the recording was done by an employee and not a "third party," the court held that the client had a reasonable expectation that her conversation was not being secretly overheard. The court further ruled that the fact that the company had informed customers at the outset of the business relationship that calls could be monitored was not adequate warning that later calls would be monitored.[30]

After this decision, plaintiffs brought many class actions alleging infringement of the CIPA through monitoring of calls between customers and businesses. Courts have dismissed some of the cases or denied class certification because plaintiffs may not have an objectively reasonable expectation of privacy because it is now well known that businesses may record calls with customer service representatives.[31]

---

[27] Ann. Cal. Penal Code § 632 *et seq.* (West) (quoting § 636); *see also Flanagan v. Flanagan*, 27 Cal. 4th 766, 774-5 (2002) (conversations are confidential if a party has an objectively reasonable expectation that conversation is not being overheard or recorded).
[28] Ann. Cal. Penal Code § 637.2 (West).
[29] *Flanagan*, 27 Cal. 4th at 772-76.
[30] *Kight v. CashCall, Inc.*, 200 Cal. App. 4th 1377, 1391-94, 1398 (2011).
[31] *Faulkner v. ADT Sec. Servs., Inc.*, 706 F.3d 1017 (9th Cir. 2013) (affirming motion to dismiss CIPA claims); *Torres v. Nutrisystem, Inc.*, 289 F.R.D. 587 (C.D. Cal. 2013) (denying motion for class certification).

Privacy of Minors

In 2013, California became the first state to enact a law governing the privacy rights of minors, which are defined as persons under eighteen years of age who reside in the state.[32] The law, which becomes effective in 2015, prohibits operators of websites, online services, online applications or mobile applications from marketing or advertising specific types of products or services to minors, including alcoholic beverages, firearms, ammunition, aerosol paint containers, tobacco products, dangerous fireworks, tanning devices, body branding, permanent tattoos, electronic cigarettes, and drug paraphernalia.[33]

The new law also requires operators to permit minors "to request and obtain removal of, content or information posted on the operator's Internet Web site, online service, online application, or mobile application by the user."[34] Operators must also provide notice to minors of their rights of access and removal of information, including notice that the removal "does not ensure complete or comprehensive removal of the content or information posted on the operator's Internet Web site, online service, online application, or mobile application by the registered user."[35] The law does not require erasure of information required by state law, posted by a third party, or of anonymized information.[36]

---

[32] Senate Bill No. 568 (adding Cal. Bus. & Prof. Code § 22580) (CA 2013).
[33] *Id.* (adding Cal. Bus. & Prof. Code § 22580(b)(1) and (i)).
[34] *Id.* (adding Cal. Bus. & Prof. Code § 22581(a)(1)).
[35] *Id.* (adding Cal. Bus. & Prof. Code § 22581(a)(4)).
[36] *Id.* (adding Cal. Bus. & Prof. Code § 22581(b)).

4

International Data Privacy and Protection Laws

Businesses today operate in a complex environment subject not only to the laws of the jurisdiction in which they have their principal place of business, but also to those where they have customers or employees. Because personal data can readily be transferred from one jurisdiction to another in digital form, it is important for businesses to be aware of the different legal regimes governing privacy and data protection that exist outside the United States so that they do not violate such laws, particularly laws relating to transfer of data from one jurisdiction to another.

Foreign privacy laws may differ considerably from those in the United States. For example, an employer may need to get the affirmative consent of an employee in the European Union for actions that could be done in the United States without any notice to, let alone consent by, the employee. Outside the United States, a person's right to protect data may trump other rights, including rights that are protected here by the First Amendment.

Two examples show the different balance struck between privacy and other rights in other countries. In Germany, where sensitivity to privacy is acute, Google encountered resistance to its Street View program, which photographs the outside of buildings and homes with traveling cameras and posts them on its Google Maps application. Although the program may have been legal under Germany's privacy laws, Google agreed to accommodate German privacy norms by pixelating some pictures of buildings in public view.[1]

---

[1] Claire Cain Miller & Kevin J. O'Brien, *Germany's Complicated Relationship with Google Street View*, N.Y. TIMES, Apr. 23, 2013, http://bits.blogs.nytimes.com/2013/04/23/germanys-complicated-relationship-with-google-street-view/.

In Hong Kong, the Privacy Commissioner for Personal Data found that a mobile app allowing users to access public litigation records that contain the names of litigants and their addresses violated the Personal Data (Privacy) Ordinance even though the information was in the public domain and was open to unrestricted use.[2] Given First Amendment freedoms, it is difficult to imagine US authorities coming to the same conclusion.

Companies should be aware of data protection laws in other countries not only if they have customers and employees in those countries, but because foreign privacy regimes may affect the development of laws in this country. Since the revelations about the data monitoring activities of the NSA, some critics have called for increased protection of privacy in the United States along the lines of existing European law. An understanding of the state of international privacy law is therefore necessary to evaluate the claims being advanced for and against different privacy regimes.

European Privacy Laws

Attention began to be paid in Europe to the protection of personal data at the same time as the United States—the 1970s. As in the United States, the reason was the growth of networked computers and databases allowing collection and sharing of large amounts of personal information about individuals. From its beginning in several West Germany states, several European countries enacted legislation governing the collection of personal information by governments and private enterprises. By 1995, when the European Data Protection Directive was enacted, the need for a more harmonized approach had become clear.

Privacy as a Fundamental Right

The European Data Protection Directive (the Directive), which is the currently applicable law governing data protection in the European Union, was enacted against a different constitutional background than exists in the United States. Unlike the United States, which does not directly refer to

---

[2] Ernest Kao & Amy Nip, *Watchdog Pulls Plug on Do No Evil App over 'Serious Invasion' of Privacy*, S. China Morning Post, Aug. 14, 2013, http://www.scmp.com/news/hong-kong/article/1296390/smartphone-app-infringes-upon-peoples-privacy-says-commission.

privacy in its Constitution, the European Union considers privacy a basic or fundamental right.

Article 8 of the European Convention on Human Rights (ECHR), which was adopted by the Council of Europe in 1950, states that "[e]veryone has the right to respect for his private and family life, his home and his correspondence" and that "[t]here shall be no interference by a public authority with the exercise of this right except such as is in accordance with the law and is necessary in a democratic society in the interests of national security, public safety or the economic well-being of the country, for the prevention of disorder or crime, for the protection of health or morals, or for the protection of the rights and freedoms of others."[3]

In 2000, the presidents of the European Parliament, the Council, and the Commission signed and proclaimed the Charter of Fundamental Rights (the Charter).[4] The Charter was given binding effect in the European Union in December 2009, when the Treaty of Lisbon came into force. The Charter broadens the right set forth in the ECHR by specifically referencing personal data. Article 8, which is headed "protection of personal data," states that:

1. Everyone has the right to the protection of personal data concerning him or her;
2. Such data must be processed fairly for specified purposes and on the basis of the consent of the person concerned or some other legitimate basis laid down by law. Everyone has the right of access to the data that has been collected concerning him or her, and the right to have it rectified; and
3. Compliance with these rules shall be subject to control by an independent authority.[5]

Although the rights in Article 8 are not absolute, they are an important underpinning for the rights to fair processing, purpose limitation,

---

[3]European Convention on Human Rights, (adopted 1950), *available at* http://www.echr.coe. int/Documents/Convention_ENG.pdf.
[4] Charter of Fundamental Rights of the European Union, (adopted 2000), *available at* http://www.europarl.europa.eu/charter/pdf/text_en.pdf.
[5] *Id.*, art. 8.

legitimate basis, access, and rectification of personal data in the EU Data Protection Directive.

The European Data Protection Directive of 1995

The Directive was enacted five years before the Charter to harmonize the protection of "data subjects" for processing data and to promote the free movement of data in the member states of the EU.[6] The Directive is enforced according to the national laws of EU member states, which are not entirely consistent. Because of these inconsistencies, the Directive may be replaced by a new data protection law that would apply uniformly to all member states.

The Directive is complex in its structure and application, but contains several important aspects:

- The Directive broadly defines personal data as "any information relating to an identified or identifiable natural person ('data subject'); an identifiable person is one who can be identified, directly or indirectly, in particular by reference to an identification number or to one or more factors specific to his physical, physiological, mental, economic, cultural or social identity."[7]
- The Directive categorizes data "revealing racial or ethnic origin, political opinions, religious or philosophical beliefs, trade-union membership, and the processing of data concerning health or sex life" as sensitive and requires greater protection for such data.[8]
- The Directive differentiates data "controllers" and "processors" and imposes greater legal obligations on controllers that "alone or jointly with others determine[] the purposes and means of the processing of personal data." In contrast, data processors, who are persons or entities that "process[] personal data on behalf of the controller," have relatively fewer obligations.[9]

---

[6] The Directive is formally known as Directive 95/46/EC of the European Parliament and of the Council on the protection of individuals with regard to the processing of personal data and on the free movement of such data [hereinafter E.U. DIRECTIVE], *available at* http://eur-lex.europa.eu/LexUriServ/LexUriServ.do?uri=CELEX:31995L0046:en:HTML.

[7] E.U. DIRECTIVE, art. 2(a).

[8] E.U. DIRECTIVE, art. 8(1).

[9] E.U. DIRECTIVE, art. 2(d)-(e).

- The Directive imposes obligations on data controllers to process data under the principles of fairness, lawfulness, purpose limitation, proportionality, and data quality.[10] Significantly, controllers can *only* process personal data under specific requirements, including a data subject's consent, compliance with legal obligations imposed on the controller, protection of the data subject's vital interests, and for purposes of "legitimate interests pursued by the data controller."[11] If the data is considered sensitive, a data subject's "explicit consent [for processing] is required."[12]

- The Directive requires that data subjects be given notice about the processing of personal data, including the identity of the controller, the purposes of the processing and further information necessary "to guarantee fair processing in respect of the data subject."[13] As a result, data subjects are typically provided information in the form of privacy notices, both for online and other types of data processing.

- The Directive gives data subjects the right to object to some data processing activities, including processing for the purpose of direct marketing.[14]

- The Directive requires controllers to "implement appropriate technical and organizational measures to protect personal data against accidental or unlawful destruction or accidental loss, alteration, unauthorized disclosure or access, in particular where the processing involves the transmission of data over a network, and against all other unlawful forms of processing."[15]

- The Directive requires establishment of national data protection authorities (DPAs) with "complete independence" that are to be notified about some processing activities and data breaches. DPAs are also given investigative and enforcement authorities concerning the Directive.[16]

- The Directive prohibits transfer of personal data from EU member states unless the country to which the data is transferred "ensures an adequate level of data protection."[17]

---

[10] E.U. DIRECTIVE, art. 6.
[11] E.U. DIRECTIVE, art. 7.
[12] E.U. DIRECTIVE, art. 8.
[13] E.U. DIRECTIVE, art. 10.
[14] E.U. DIRECTIVE, art. 14.
[15] E.U. DIRECTIVE, art. 17.
[16] E.U. DIRECTIVE, art. 28.
[17] E.U. DIRECTIVE, art. 25(1).

The Directive is broader in scope than any national or state data protection law in the United States. It is a baseline law specifying limited grounds for lawful processing of personal data by data controllers. The Directive is thus not limited to any specific sector (such as health care) or type of personal information (such as "protected health information"), but applies to *all types and forms of personal data.*

Unlike US law, the Directive requires all data controllers to process data only under specific principles (similar to the FIPPs). If the processing *does not meet one of the criteria*—such as consent or the data controller's "legitimate interests"—it cannot be processed.

"Data subjects," which is broader than "consumers" protected under the FTC Act, are given rights to control the processing of information that many of their US counterparts do not have. Although individuals in the United States may be given information about processing of information through online privacy notices, the information provided in the European Union is both more detailed and is provided under a greater number of circumstances.

A major difference between EU and US law is the role of the data protection authority or DPA. The FTC has a somewhat similar role in regard to some US laws, but is not entirely equivalent to a DPA. A DPA's authority is not only broader, but more proscriptive, since it may require companies to apply for consent to process data. A final important difference is that EU law prohibits the transfer of information outside of the European Economic Area, which includes the European Union and some other European countries, unless the transferee country has "adequate" data protection. Few countries have been determined to be "adequate," and the United States is not one of those countries.

The EU/US Safe Harbor

Because the Directive would have "significantly hampered the ability of U.S. organizations to engage in a range of trans-Atlantic transactions," the US Department of Commerce, working with the European Commission, developed a "safe harbor" framework.[18] By joining this

---

[18] Department of Commerce, *U.S.-EU Safe Harbor Overview*, http://export.gov/safeharbor/eu/eg_main_018476.asp.

voluntary program and adhering to its principles through public declaration and adopting a privacy program incorporating these principles, US businesses are deemed to have "adequate" privacy protections and the requirements of EU member states for prior approval of data transfers are not applicable. Moreover, claims brought by EU citizens against US organizations will be heard in the United States.[19]

Organizations joining the Safe Harbor must follow seven "Safe Harbor Principles":

- Notice. Organizations must notify individuals about the purposes for which they collect and use information about them. They must provide information about how individuals can contact the organization with any inquiries or complaints, the types of third parties to which it discloses the information, and the choices and means the organization offers for limiting its use and disclosure.

- Choice. Organizations must give individuals the opportunity to choose (opt out) whether their personal information will be disclosed to a third party or used for a purpose incompatible with the purpose for which it was originally collected or subsequently authorized by the individual. For sensitive information, affirmative or explicit (opt in) choice must be given if the information is to be disclosed to a third party or used for a purpose other than its original purpose or the purpose authorized subsequently by the individual.

- Onward Transfer (Transfers to Third Parties). To disclose information to a third party, organizations must apply the notice and choice principles. Where an organization wishes to transfer information to a third party that is acting as an agent, it may do so if it makes sure that the third party subscribes to the Safe Harbor Privacy Principles or is subject to the Directive or another adequacy finding. As an alternative, the organization can enter into a written agreement with such third party requiring that the third party provide at least the same level of privacy protection as is required by the relevant principles.

---

[19] *Id.*

- Access. Individuals must have access to personal information about them that an organization holds and be able to correct, amend, or delete that information where it is inaccurate, except where the burden or expense of providing access would be disproportionate to the risks to the individual's privacy in the case in question, or where the rights of persons other than the individual would be violated.

- Security. Organizations must take reasonable precautions to protect personal information from loss, misuse and unauthorized access, disclosure, alteration, and destruction.

- Data integrity. Personal information must be relevant for the purposes for which it is to be used. An organization should take reasonable steps to ensure that data is reliable for its intended use, accurate, complete, and current.

- Enforcement. In order to ensure compliance with the safe harbor principles, there must be (a) readily available and affordable independent recourse mechanisms so that each individual's complaints and disputes can be investigated and resolved and damages awarded where the applicable law or private sector initiatives so provide; (b) procedures for verifying that the commitments companies make to adhere to the safe harbor principles have been implemented; and (c) obligations to remedy problems arising out of a failure to comply with the principles. Sanctions must be sufficiently rigorous to ensure compliance by the organization. Organizations that fail to provide annual self-certification letters will no longer appear in the list of participants and safe harbor benefits will no longer be assured.[20]

The FTC enforces Safe Harbor Principles for most businesses and the Department of Transportation for airlines. The FTC enforces the failure to follow Safe Harbor Principles under Section 5 of the FTC Act as "deceptive" practices. The FTC in 2009 settled actions with six companies that falsely claimed membership in the program.[21] Under the settlement,

---

[20] Id.
[21] Press Release, Federal Trade Commission, *FTC Settles with Six Companies Claiming to Comply with International Privacy Framework*, Oct. 6, 2009, http://www.ftc.gov/opa/2009/10/safeharbor.shtm.

the companies were "prohibited from misrepresenting the extent to which they participate in any privacy, security, or other compliance program sponsored by a government or any third party."[22]

The 2012 Proposed EU Data Protection Regulation

On January 25, 2012, the European Commission published a proposal for a General Data Protection Regulation (Proposed Regulation).[23] If passed by the European Parliament and Council, the Proposed Regulation would be binding on EU member states and replace the Directive. The Proposed Regulation has been called "the most significant global development in data protection law since the EU Data Protection Directive . . ."[24]

In the months after the Proposed Regulation was announced, there was considerable debate over the proposed changes to the EU data protection regime both internally and externally. At the time of this writing (Summer 2013), a committee of the European Parliament is considering thousands of proposed amendments to the Proposed Regulation and there is no final text for the law. Once passed by the European Council and Parliament, the Proposed Regulation would not take effect for two years. Despite these uncertainties, it is likely that the Proposed Regulation will change and strengthen European privacy protections in ways that will affect businesses operating in or having businesses dealings with the European Union.

There are significant differences between the Proposed Regulation and the current Directive:

- Because the law is styled as a "regulation" and not a "directive," it will have direct and uniform effect on all EU member states without the necessity of implementing legislation by the states;

---

[22] Id.

[23] European Commission, Proposal for General Data Protection Regulation [hereinafter E.U. PROPOSED REG.], Jan. 25, 2012, http://ec.europa.eu/justice/data-protection/document/review 2012/com_2012_11_en.pdf.

[24] Jane Finlayson-Brown, *How to Prepare for the Proposed EU Data Protection Regulation*, COMPUTERWEEKLY.COM, Mar. 2012, http://www.computerweekly.com/ opinion/Proposed-EU-Data-Protection-Regulation-what-should-companies-be-thinking-about.

- The Proposed Regulation will affect a broader range of companies than the Directive because it applies not only to controllers and processors located in the EU but also to those outside the EU that offer goods or services to data subjects in the EU or monitor their behavior.[25]

- The Proposed Regulation tightens the conditions by which consent is obtained for data processing and generally provides a greater level of data protection for EU residents. Consent may not be a legal basis for processing where there is a "significant imbalance between the position of the data subject and the controller" as in the employment relationship.[26] Rights of notice and access by data subjects are also expanded.

- The Proposed Regulation establishes a single regulatory authority for compliance by entities—the so-called "one-stop shop." In contrast to the current Directive, an entity will only have to obtain consent from a single DPA, instead of from multiple authorities.[27]

- The Proposed Regulation has a uniform mechanism granting significantly greater penalties and enforcement powers to DPAs, including graduated fines of up to €1,000,000 or up to 2 percent of annual global sales for intentional or negligent violations.[28]

- The Proposed Regulation increases responsibilities of data controllers for data security and encourages "privacy by design."[29]

- Companies with more than 250 employees must appoint a data protection officer (DPO).[30]

- Data controllers must notify DPAs "without undue delay and, where feasible, not later than 24 hours after having become aware" of a data breach.[31]

- The Proposed Regulation includes a "right to be forgotten"— erasure of personal data when an individual withdraws consent, objects to processing personal data, and when data is no longer necessary or there is no "legitimate reason" for a company to keep the data.[32] The "right to be forgotten" applies even if data has been made public.

---

[25] E.U. PROPOSED REG., art. 3.
[26] E.U. PROPOSED REG., art. 5, art. 7, recital 34.
[27] E.U. PROPOSED REG., art. 51.
[28] E.U. PROPOSED REG., art. 79.
[29] E.U. PROPOSED REG., art. 30.
[30] E.U. PROPOSED REG., art. 35.
[31] E.U. PROPOSED REG., art. 31.
[32] E.U. PROPOSED REG., art. 17.

- The Proposed Regulation improves mechanisms for transferring data out of the EU, including binding corporate rules.[33]

Even if the text of the Proposed Regulation is not yet settled and it will be some years before it comes into effect, it represents a significant change for data protection rights that may reverberate outside of the European Union. US interests have actively lobbied the EU to eliminate or change requirements that they believe would be onerous or anti-competitive.[34] In response to these lobbying efforts, some EU Parliament members have called for even stricter controls for consent by data subjects for services of companies having a "dominant market position" or engaging in online advertising.[35]

Since the revelations about the NSA's surveillance operations, European criticism of the perceived lack of privacy protections in the United States has increased. In late November 2013, the EU issued a report that criticized the Safe Harbor and offered suggestions for improvement of the mechanism.[36] As the former director of the program has noted, European criticism of the Safe Harbor program—which remains the law—may be prompted as much by the "dominance of U.S. multinationals...of the high technology sector in Europe and the U.S." as it is by any other factor.[37]

North American Privacy Laws.

Canada

Canada has two federal privacy laws, the Privacy Act—which applies to federal government departments—and the Personal Information Protection and Electronic Documents Act (PIPEDA) —which applies to the private sector.[38] PIPEDA governs the ways in which organizations collect, use or

---

[33] E.U. PROPOSED REG., art. 41-43.

[34] Timothy J. Toohey, *Why Google Could Start a Trade War over Europe's Privacy Rules*, USA TODAY, Mar. 22, 2013, *available at* http://www.usatoday.com/story/tech/2013/03/22/europe-privacy-laws-google-facebook-trade-war/2010643/.

[35] *Id.*

[36] European Commission, Press Release, *Restoring Trust in EU-US data flows—Frequently Asked Questions*, http://europa.eu/rapid/press-release_MEMO-13-1059_en.htm.

[37] Damon Greer, *Safe Harbor May be Controversial in the European Union, But It Is Still the Law*, IAPP Privacy Advisor, Aug. 27, 2013, https://www.privacyassociation.org/publications/safe_harbor_may_be_controversial_in_the_european_union_but_it_is_still_the.

[38] Office of the Privacy Commissioner of Canada, *Fact Sheets: Privacy Legislation in Canada*, http://www.priv.gc.ca/resource/fs-fi/02_05_d_15_e.asp.

disclose personal information in the course of commercial activities and provides individuals with a right to access and correct personal information. Similar to the EU Directive, PIPEDA requires that there be a lawful basis for collecting personal information.[39] In addition, Canadian provinces and territories have laws relating to collection of information by government departments. PIPEDA does not apply to personal information of employees of provincially regulated organizations.[40] Some have criticized PIPEDA for not including a comprehensive data breach notification regime and for the inadequate enforcement powers given to the Privacy Commissioner.[41]

Mexico

The Mexican law on the Protection of Personal Data Held by Private Parties came into effect on July 6, 2010. The law requires that there be a lawful basis for collecting, processing, using, and disclosing personal information.[42] The law tracks the EU model in some respects providing notice to people about processing and rights of access, correction, and objection.[43] As in some other Latin American countries, the Mexican data protection law is based on the concept of "habeas data," which gives "individuals the right to access, correct, and object to the processing of their information" to protect "image, privacy, honor, self-determination of information and freedom of information."[44]

Asian and Australian Privacy Laws

Asian privacy laws vary considerably. Hong Kong, Singapore, and South Korea have stronger privacy laws than other Asian countries. India and Thailand are considering privacy bills, but have not yet enacted legislation.[45]

---

[39] *Id.*

[40] *Id.*

[41] Press Release, Canadian Internet Policy and Public Interest Clinic, *Private Member Bill Seeks to Bring Long Overdue Privacy Protections for Canadians*, Feb. 27, 2013, https://www.cippic.ca/en/news/PMB_PIPEDA_Order_Making_Powers.

[42] W. Scott Blackmer, *Mexico's New Data Protection Law,* Information LawGroup, Jul. 28, 2010, http://www.infolawgroup.com/2010/07/articles/privacy-law/mexicos-new-data-protection-law/.

[43] *Id.*

[44] *Id.; see also* Department of International Law, Organization of American States, *Data Protection*, http://www.oas.org/dil/data_protection_privacy_habeas_data.htm.

[45] Information Shield, *International Privacy Laws*, http://www.informationshield.com/int privacylaws.html.

Hong Kong's Personal Data (Privacy) Ordinance, which was amended in 2012, requires a lawful purpose for data collection. An independent body called the Office of Privacy Commissioner for Personal Data enforces the law. The Ordinance requires that "personal data shall be collected for a purpose directly related to a function and activity of the data user," that data collection be "lawful and fair," and that "data subjects shall be informed of the purpose for which the data are collected and to be used."[46] As a result of the 2012 amendments, businesses using personal data for direct marketing purposes are required to inform data subjects and provide them with a means to say whether they object to the intended use of the information.[47]

China has no comprehensive national legislation governing data privacy, nor does it have a national data protection agency. In recent years, China has enacted or proposed some measures strengthening protection of online information. China's Ministry of Industry and Information Technology, which regulates Chinese Internet service providers, has also issued non-binding guidelines for organizations that collect, use, and disclose personal information, including requiring express consent for processing sensitive data and cross-border transfers of any personal information.[48] Some view these measures as a potential harbinger of a comprehensive Chinese data protection initiative that may restrict cross-border transfers.[49]

Australia has both a national Privacy Act and state privacy laws. The Privacy Act regulates personal information about individuals and includes principles relating to handling of personal information by public agencies and by large businesses, health service providers, and some other businesses and organizations.[50] The principles applying to enterprises include principles

[46] Office of the Privacy Commissioner for Personal Data, *Six Data Protection Principles (DPP) of the Personal Data (Privacy) Ordinacy*, http://www.pcpd.org.hk/english/ordinance/ordglance.html.
[47] Office of the Privacy Commissioner for Personal Data, Hong Kong, *An Overview of the Major Provisions of the Personal Data (Privacy) (Amendment) Ordinance 2012*, Sept. 2012, http://www.pcpd.org.hk/english/publications/files/ordinance2012_overview_e.pdf.
[48] Hogan Lovells Privacy Team, *Making Sense of China's New Privacy Laws*, IAPP Privacy Tracker, Jun. 28, 2013, https://www.privacyassociation.org/privacy_tracker/post/making_sense_of_chinas_new_privacy_laws.
[49] *Id.*
[50] Office of the Australian Information Commissioner, *The Privacy Act*, http://www.oaic.gov.au/privacy/privacy-act/the-privacy-act.

for collection, use and disclosure, information quality and security, openness, access and correction, identifiers, anonymity, transborder data flows, and sensitive information.

Significant amendments to the Privacy Act that will take effect on March 12, 2014 include new harmonized Australian Privacy Principles pertaining to:

- Open and transparent management of personal information;
- Anonymity and pseudonymity;
- Solicited personal information;
- Unsolicited personal information;
- Notification of the collection of personal information;
- Use or disclosure of personal information;
- Direct marketing;
- Cross-border disclosure of personal information;
- Adoption, use or disclosure of government related identifiers;
- Quality of personal information;
- Security of personal information;
- Access to personal information; and
- Correction of personal information.[51]

International Privacy Frameworks

Besides national privacy frameworks, cross-border transfers of personal information may be facilitated by voluntary international privacy frameworks. One of the frameworks recently gaining prominence is the privacy framework developed by the Asia-Pacific Economic Cooperation (APEC) entity.[52] The framework is designed to:

- Improve information sharing among government agencies and regulators;
- Facilitate the safe transfer of information between economies;

---

[51] Office of the Australian Information Commissioner, *Privacy Fact Sheet 17: Australian Privacy Principles*, Feb. 2013, http://www.oaic.gov.au/images/documents/privacy/privacy-resources/privacy-fact-sheets/privacy-fact-sheet-17-australian-privacy-principles.pdf.
[52] APEC members include all the major North American and Asian economies, including the United States, Mexico, China, and Thailand, as well as some South American economies.

- Establish a common set of privacy principles;
- Encourage the use of electronic data as a means to enhance and expand business; and
- Provide technical assistance to those economies that have yet to address privacy from a regulatory or policy perspective.[53]

APEC has also adopted a system of voluntary cross-border privacy rules for the APEC region called the APEC Cross-Border Privacy Rules (CBPR) System.[54] Organizations putting those privacy policies into effect are evaluated by a third party to ensure compliance with the cross-border system. Once an organization has been certified, the policies and practices are binding on the business and are enforced by an authority, such as a regulator, to ensure compliance with program requirements.[55] In August 2013, IBM became the first company to receive certification under the CBPR system.[56]

---

[53] Asia-Pacific Economic Cooperation, *APEC Data Privacy Pathfinder*, http://www.apec.org/ About-Us/About-APEC/Fact-Sheets/APEC-Privacy-Framework.aspx.

[54] *See generally* Asia-Pacific Economic Cooperation, APEC Cross-Border Privacy Rules System, http://www.apec.org/Groups/Committee-on-Trade-and-Investment/~/media/Files/ Groups/ ECSG/CBPR/CBPR-PoliciesRulesGuidelines.ashx.

[55] *Id.* at 3.

[56] Press Release, IBM, I*BM Becomes First Company Certified Under APEC Cross Border Privacy Rules*, Aug. 12, 2013, http://www-03.ibm.com/press/us/en/pressrelease/41760.wss.

5

Privacy Issues in the Workplace

Data privacy issues may emerge in all stages of the employment relationship, including before, during, and after employment. Besides federal anti-discrimination laws, such as the Civil Rights Act, the Americans with Disabilities Act, and the Age Discrimination Act and Equal Pay Act that protect some aspects of employee privacy, both US federal and state governments have enacted specific laws dealing with privacy in the workplace.

Privacy issues in the employment context also arise from a wide variety of factual circumstances, including background screening, monitoring of employee communications, testing for substance abuse, use of social media sites, and employee use of electronic devices. The blurring between the workplace and home made possible by technologies such as smartphones, tablets and high-speed Internet connections has affected employee expectations of privacy and is likely to continue to do so in the future.

Pre-Employment Screening

As part of the background screening or other employment decisions, employers may use consumer reports from consumer reporting agencies to assess employees. Employers using these reports must comply with the Fair Credit Reporting Act (FCRA).

FCRA requires an employer to get written permission from employees and applicants before asking for a report from a consumer reporting agency. The employer must provide written notice to the person that it is obtaining a consumer report and that it might use that information to make a decision relating to employment. The information must be in a stand-alone form and not part of an employment application. Moreover, the employer must certify to the company from which it is getting the report that it has notified the applicant or employee, has complied with FCRA, and will not discriminate against the employee or misuse the information.[1]

Before an employer takes "adverse action," such as rejecting a job application or terminating an employee, it must also give the person notice that includes a copy of the consumer report relied on to make the decision and a copy of the FTC's *A Summary of Your Rights under the Fair Credit Reporting Act*.[2] The purpose of this requirement is to allow the applicant or employee to correct the information in the report. After taking adverse action, an employer must give the affected individual notice orally, in writing, or electronically. The notice must include information relating to the consumer reporting agency, a statement that the company making the report did not make the decision, and that the person has the right to dispute the accuracy or completeness of the information.[3] The employer must also securely dispose of consumer reports.[4]

States have also enacted laws affecting background and investigative reports. Under California's Investigative Consumer Reporting Agencies Act, job applicants have greater rights than under FCRA to see the results of an investigative consumer report, which is a report "in which information on a consumer's character, general reputation, personal characteristics, or mode of living is obtained through any means."[5] In contrast, FCRA does not treat communications to employers of investigations of suspected misconduct by an employee as consumer reports, but does require employers to provide employees with a summary of the nature and substance of communications upon which adverse actions are based.[6]

---

[1] Federal Trade Commission, *Using Consumer Reports: What Employers Need to Know*, Jan. 2012, http://business.ftc.gov/documents/bus08-using-consumer-reports-what-employers-need-know.

[2] *Id*; *see also* Federal Trade Commission, *A Summary of Your Rights Under the Fair Credit Reporting Act*, http://www.consumer.ftc.gov/sites/default/files/articles/pdf/pdf-0096-fair-credit-reporting-act.pdf.

[3] *See Using Consumer Reports supra* n. 1.

[4] Federal Trade Commission, *Disposing of Consumer Report Information? New Rule Tells How*, Jun. 2005, http://business.ftc.gov/documents/alt152-disposing-consumer-report-information-new-rule-tells-how.

[5] Ann. Cal. Civ. Code §§ 1786 *et seq.* (West).

[6] 15 U.S.C. § 1681a(y) (West).

Employee Privacy Expectations

Rapidly changing technology has changed the workplace dramatically in the last decades. The use of personal computers, tablets, and mobile devices, such as smartphones, has increased exponentially. With the use of such devices, employers have greater ability to monitor employees both in and outside the workplace. Employees, however, also have the ability to work remotely, rather than at the workplace. The pervasive use of social media, including Facebook or LinkedIn, the ready availability of web-accessed e-mail accounts, including Hotmail or Gmail, and the use by employees of private devices in the workplace have also complicated employers' governance of the workplace.

The "consumerization" of information technology—the phenomenon in which technology emerges in the consumer marketplace and then migrates to the workplace (as opposed to a "top down" approach)—has also had a significant effect on privacy expectations. The authors of a study on consumerization have written that "[m]any employees now have significantly more capable devices and services at home than those provided in the workplace."[7] These technological trends will likely continue to have an effect on both employees and employers.

Employee Monitoring

Employee monitoring by employers is relatively prevalent in the United States, including monitoring of telephone calls, Internet usage, and performance. Employers also track employees through security access to the workplace, call recording, mandatory drug testing, and employee use of social media to detect security threats. A drugstore chain even announced recently that employees using the company's insurance plan would have to report their weight, height, body fat, blood pressure, and glucose levels or face a $600 noncompliance penalty.[8]

---

[7] John Taylor, *The 'Consumerization' of Information Technology Position Paper*, 2, CSC Research & Advisory Services, http://lef.csc.com/projects/70.

[8] Christine McConville, *CVS Presses Workers for Medical Information*, Bostonherald.com Biz Smart, Mar. 19, 2013, http://bostonherald.com/business/healthcare/2013/03/cvs_presses_workers_for_medical_information.

Unlike the European Union, employees in the United States are often said to have diminished expectations of privacy in the workplace. Several reasons are typically given for workers' diminished privacy, including the lack of constitutional privacy protections, the lack of state laws protecting employees, and employer policies and procedures restricting employees' use of computer equipment in the workplace.

The recent United States Supreme Court case of *City of Ontario v. Quon* illustrates some of the legal dimensions of the issue.[9] In *Quon*, the city monitored a policeman's text messages and found that many messages were not work related and were sexually explicit. The city concluded that the policeman had violated internal usage rules and that the messages were not private because "[u]sers should have no expectation of privacy or confidentiality" when using the city's computers.

Although the Supreme Court concluded that employees do not lose their Fourth Amendment rights by virtue of working for the government, it nonetheless found that the city's search was reasonable because it was "motivated by a legitimate work-related purpose, and because it was not excessive in scope."[10] Despite this ruling, the Supreme Court stopped short of expressing any hard and fast view about "the whole concept of privacy expectations in communications made on electronic equipment owned by a government employer."

The Supreme Court wrote that "[r]apid changes in the dynamics of communication and information transmission" are affecting views about the use of computer equipment by employees and that employers "expect or at least tolerate personal use of such equipment by employees because it often increases worker efficiency." The Court further said that "[c]ell phone and text message communications are so pervasive that some persons may consider them to be essential means or necessary instruments for self-expression, even self-identification."[11]

Despite the nuanced views expressed in *Quon*, courts have ruled that employees do not have a reasonable expectation of privacy in e-mail

---

[9] *City of Ontario, Cal. v. Quon*, 130 S. Ct. 2619 (2010).
[10] *Id.* at 2632-33.
[11] *Id.* at 2629-30.

messages sent over work computers. A California court in 2002 held that an employee who had been given a computer to permit him to work at home and who refused to turn over the computer when he was terminated for "repeatedly accessing pornographic sites on the Internet while he was at work" had no reasonable expectation of privacy when using the computer for personal matters.[12] The court rejected the employee's privacy claim because the employee knew that his employer would monitor the files and messages stored on the computers he used at the office and at home.[13] The court also found that the employee had "voluntarily waived whatever right of privacy he might otherwise have had in the information he stored on the home computer."[14]

Employee expectations about privacy continue to evolve as mobile devices, tablets, and other technology have made it easier to access websites and private e-mail accounts at work. Recognizing changing technology and expectations, a court concluded that an employer violated the Stored Communications Act (SCA) when it accessed personal e-mail messages from an employee's web-based e-mail service. The fact that the employer had a computer use policy in its employee handbook stating that e-mail users had "no right of personal privacy in any matter stored in, created on, received from, or sent through or over the system," including "personal e-mail accounts," was insufficient to infer that the employee consented to accessing e-mails "maintained by outside entities such as Microsoft or Google."[15]

Social Media

Social media sites allowing users to interact with one another and post content are prominent features of the Web 2.0 world. Sites such as Facebook and LinkedIn present privacy issues to employers and employees alike, as seen by these examples:

---

[12] *TBG Ins. Servs. Corp. v. Superior Court*, 96 Cal. App. 4th 443, 446 (2002).

[13] *Id.* at 453.

[14] *Id.* at 454.

[15] *Pure Power Boot Camp v. Warrior Fitness Boot Camp*, 587 F. Supp. 2d 548, 559 (S.D.N.Y. 2008) (finding employer's access of former employees' e-mails violated the SCA); *see also Pure Power Boot Camp, Inc. v. Warrior Fitness Boot Camp, LLC*, 759 F. Supp. 2d 417, 429-30 (S.D.N.Y. 2010) (finding four violations of SCA committed and awarding $1,000 per violation).

- An employer requires an employee to disclose a username or password to access the employee's social media account for purposes of a workplace investigation;

- An employee establishes a social media account for her employer but refuses to provide the account password when she is terminated from employment;

- An employee uses a social media account displaying his employer's name or brand to make disparaging comments about a public figure; and

- An employer has a policy prohibiting discussions of information about the company on a social media site and takes action against an employee as a result of critical postings.

The first example, where employers have asked employees to provide them with social media passwords, has led to several state laws prohibiting the practice. California in 2012 enacted laws restricting access by schools to "personal" social media accounts and by employers to employees' social media accounts.[16] Both laws define "social media" broadly as "an electronic service or account, or electronic content, including, but not limited to, videos, still photographs, blogs, video blogs, podcasts, instant and text messages, e-mail, online services or accounts, or Internet Web site profiles or accounts." Because the laws do not define "personal" social media, complications arise when a social networking site is used for both business and personal purposes.[17] Despite these laws, some employers continue to monitor employee use of social media to detect security threats.

Mixed use of social media accounts can lead not only to unclear laws, but to lawsuits. In a recent case, a terminated employee refused to turn over login credentials for a blog she had maintained for her employer.[18]

---

[16] *See* Ann. Cal. Educ. Code §§ 99120-22 (West); *see also* Cal. Labor Code § 980 (West).

[17] Eric Goldman, *Big Problems in California's New Law Restricting Employers' Access to Employees' Online Accounts*, FORBES, Sept. 28, 2012, http://www.forbes.com/sites/ericgold man/2012/09/28/big-problems-in-californias-new-law-restricting-employers-access-to-employees-online-accounts/.

[18] Venkat Balasubramani, *Fight Over Access to Log-in Credentials for Blog Does Not Trigger Copyright Preemption – Insynq v. Mann*, Technology & Marketing Law Blog, Sept. 7, 2012, http://blog.ericgoldman.org/archives/2012/09/access_to_login.htm.

In another lawsuit, former business partners battled over the ownership of a LinkedIn account and phone number.[19] An employee also sued her employer for accessing her social media accounts during her absence from work due to an accident.[20] And finally, members of a political group fought one another in court about who owned the group's trademarks and social media accounts.[21]

Although lawsuits over the ownership of social media accounts arise under a variety of legal theories—from misappropriation of assets to trademark and copyright infringement—the disputes show the blurring of the personal and business-related aspects of the online world. Social media sites affect the privacy of personal data not only because they allow people to share information that otherwise may not be publicly disclosed, but also because they create difficult issues of access and ownership. Employees maintaining social media sites that comment on or promote their work may feel that they have a vested personal ownership in such sites that is at odds with their employers' views.

Employees with access to company Twitter feeds may also create problems for their employers if the accounts are misused. When an employee with access to a corporate account tweeted a tasteless joke during a presidential debate, the company was the focus of considerable adverse publicity. Although the company immediately deleted the account, it had to apologize that a member of its "Twitter team mistakenly posted an offensive tweet from the [company's] handle instead of a personal handle."[22]

Restrictions in companies' "acceptable use" policies for social media accounts may address some of these issues of ownership and misuse of

---

[19] Venkat Balasubramani, *Another Set of Parties Duel Over Social Media Contacts – Eagle v. Sawabeh*, Technology & Marketing Law Blog, Dec. 28, 2011, http://blog.ericgoldman.org/archives/2011/12/another_set_of_1.htm.

[20] Venkat Balasubramani, *Employee's Claims Against Employer for Unauthorized Use of Social Media Accounts Move Forward—Maremont v. SF Design Group*, Technology & Marketing Blog, Dec. 8, 2011, http://blog.ericgoldman.org/archives/2011/12/ maremont_v_sfg.htm.

[21] Eric Goldman, *Tea Partiers Wage War Against Each Other Over a Google Groups Account — Kremer v. Tea Party Patriots*, Technology & Marketing Blog, Mar. 2, 2012, http://blog.ericgoldman.org/archives/2012/03/tea_partiers_ba.htm.

[22] Prachi Gupta, *Kitchen Aid Insults Obama's Grandma*, SALON, Oct. 4, 2012, http://www.salon.com/2012/10/04/kitchenaid_insults_obamas_grandma/.

company accounts for personal purposes. Yet some of these policies may also violate National Labor Relations Board (NLRB) guidelines that prohibit policies that undermine the ability of employees to speak and act together to address work conditions. The NLRB has said that social media rules "prohibiting employees from posting information regarding the [e]mployer that could be deemed 'confidential' or 'non-public'" are unlawful because they are "so vague that employees would reasonably construe it to include subjects that involve their working conditions."[23]

Bring Your Own Device (BYOD)

The blurring of the personal and private also impacts employees' use of technology in the workplace. In response to employee demand, many employers have gone from providing devices to their workers to allowing them to access business applications and information from their own devices. For example, IBM, which previously had a "corporate managed mobile-phone plan that historically...focused on BlackBerries," has adopted a BYOD (Bring Your Own Device) approach for the company's 440,000 employees.[24] As the chief information officer of IBM said, the BYOD program was "'really...about supporting employees in the way they want to work...They will find the most appropriate tool to get their job done. I want to make sure I can enable them to do that, but in a way that safeguards the integrity of our business.'"[25]

From the employer's point of view, BYOD challenges the security of a business' proprietary and confidential information. When it owns devices, an employer has an easier time enforcing proper use guidelines. If a device is stolen, it can remotely wipe and replace it. In a BYOD world, matters are more complex.

An employee who uses a device bought with his or her own money (even if subsidized by an employer) may not want to have personal information

---

[23] National Labor Relations Board Advice Memorandum Re Giant Food LLC, 10, Mar. 21, 2012, http://www.employmentlawwatch.com/uploads/file/July%202013%20Advice%20 Memorandum.pdf

[24] Chris Kanaracus, *IBM CIO discusses Big Blue's BYOD strategy*, COMPUTER WORLD, Mar. 26, 2012, http://www.computerworld.com/s/article/9225563/ IBM_CIO_discusses_Big_Blue_ 39_s_BYOD_strategy.

[25] *Id.*

accessed or erased by the employer. The employee may also use the same mobile phone by which she accesses work e-mails to store information about a health condition (which would be protected health information under HIPAA), financial transactions (which would be nonpublic financial information under GLB) or personal photos or movies. A survey found that 46 percent of people in the United States would feel "violated" by the news that their personal data was accessed by their IT department.[26]

Other privacy issues may arise for employer-owned devices. For example, the Computer Fraud and Abuse Act (CFAA), which has been used to prosecute *employees* who use employer computer systems to transmit information belonging to the employers, may be used against *employers* who gain unauthorized access to a computer. If an employer remotely wipes personal data from a device, the employee may bring a lawsuit, particularly if the employee is discharged. As earlier mentioned, an employer may also be legally responsible under the SCA if it accesses an employee's private e-mail account.[27]

---

[26] Aruba Networks, *Employees Tell the Truth About Your Company's Data*, 2013, http://www.arubanetworks.com/pdf/solutions/EB_mdmreport.pdf.
[27] *Pure Power Boot Camp, supra* n. 11.

6

Data Security and Data Breaches

It has been quipped that there can be security without privacy but no privacy without security. The best security in the world will not protect private information if there are no controls for consent, collection, and processing. Conversely, even if every jot and tittle of privacy requirements are followed, they mean nothing if personal information is not securely maintained. Otherwise put, privacy is the goal and security is the means to that goal.

Security Challenges and Costs

Security risks extend well beyond personal data, such as social security or bank account numbers. Unauthorized attacks also seek valuable corporate and government data, including patents, trade secrets, and strategic plans. Private and state-sponsored hackers, malware programs, phishing and spear-phishing attacks, Distributed Denial of Service (DDoS) attacks, social engineering attacks, and many other malicious incursions are directed to these digital corporate assets. In 2013, DDoS attacks have brought down several US banks and firms, *The New York Times*, and the Chinese Internet.

Somewhat ironically, given the attack on the Chinese Internet, a report in *The New York Times* in 2013 revealed that a white office tower in Shanghai housed a People's Liberation Army base responsible for "an overwhelming percentage of the attacks on American corporations, organizations and government agencies..."[1] A later article on hacker

---

[1] David E. Sanger, David Barboza & Nicole Perlroth, *Chinese Army Unit is Seen as Tied to Hacking Against U.S.*, N.Y. TIMES, Feb. 18, 2013, *available at* http://www.nytimes.com/2013/02/19/technology/chinas-army-is-seen-as-tied-to-hacking-against-us.html?pagewanted=all.

culture in China said that "[s]ome hackers see crime as more lucrative than legitimate work, but opportunities for skilled hackers to earn generous salaries abound, given the growing number of cybersecurity companies providing network defense services to the government, state-owned enterprises and private companies."[2] The head of the New York FBI unit in charge of defending against cyberattacks has also cited "[d]estructive capabilities of certain nation-states" as a top emerging threat.[3]

China does not have a monopoly on hacking US government and private enterprise computers. In what was called the "biggest cybercrime spree yet," federal officials indicted five Russians and a Ukrainian for stealing 160 million credit card numbers to rob financial firms through a Structured Query Language (SQL) injection attack.[4] Others actors, including "hactivists" espousing social causes, have attacked major corporations and even the US government.

Contrary to some perceptions, unauthorized attacks on computer systems do not necessarily require sophisticated technical knowledge or advanced hacking techniques. It is now possible for would-be hackers without programming abilities to buy ready-made kits to cobble together malware programs to attack computer networks. A 2013 study of 621 confirmed data breaches conducted by nineteen global organizations said that "breaches are a multi-faceted problem, and any one-dimensional attempt to describe them fails to adequately capture their complexity."[5] The report found that 92 percent of breaches in 2012 were committed by outsiders to the organization and that 19 percent of breaches were attributed to state-affiliated actors, principally China;[6] 55 percent of

---

[2] Edward Wong, *Hackers Find China is Land of Opportunity*, N.Y. TIMES, May 22, 2013, *available at* http://www.nytimes.com/2013/05/23/world/asia/in-china-hacking-has-widespread-acceptance.html?pagewanted=all.
[3] Andrew Tangel, *FBI agent Austin Berglas fights cyberattacks on corporate america*, L.A. TIMES, Sept. 20, 2013, *available at* http://www.latimes.com/business/la-fi-0921-fbi-cyber-qa-20130921,0,3321489.story.
[4] E. Scott Reckard & Paresh Dave, *Russians indicted in giant hacking scheme*, L.A. TIMES, Jul. 26, 2013, *available at* http://articles.latimes.com/2013/jul/26/ business/la-fi-hacking-charges-20130726.
[5] Verizon, *2013 Data Breach Investigations Report*, 4, *available at* http://www.verizon enterprise.com/DBIR/2013/.
[6] *Id.* at 5.

breaches involved organized crime, 2 percent activists, and one percent former employees.[7]

The report further found that 52 percent of the breaches used some form of hacking, 76 percent were network incursions exploiting weak or stolen credentials, 40 percent used malware, 35 percent involved physical attacks, 29 percent leveraged social engineering tactics, and 13 percent resulted from privilege misuse and abuse.[8] Perhaps the most remarkable conclusion is that 10 percent of breaches involved a "very low" level of skill, 68 percent a "low" level, 22 percent a "moderate" level, and less than one percent a "high" level.[9] As the report said, "it's really not all that surprising that none [of the breaches] receive the highly difficult rating. Would you fire a guided missile at an unlocked screen door?"[10]

Despite the relatively low level of skill needed to accomplish 78 percent of the 2012 breaches, the incursions exact large costs. A July 2013 study of the Economic Impact of Cybercrime and Cyber Espionage estimates that the cost of US cyber activity is between $24 and $120 billion, consisting of loss of intellectual property, direct financial losses, loss of sensitive business information, opportunity costs, costs of securing networks, expenses to recover from cyber-attacks, and reputational damage to the hacked company.[11]

Another study analyzing the cost of data breaches puts the average cost in 2012 of a data breach in the United States at $188 per record and the average number of breached records at 28,765 per breach. The study also estimates that the average total organizational cost of a data breach in the United States is $5,403,644.[12] Although these figures are subject to qualifications, they show that data breaches are pervasive and expensive.

---

[7] *Id*. at 21.

[8] *Id*. at 6.

[9] *Id*. at 48-9.

[10] *Id*. at 49.

[11] Center for Strategic & International Studies, *The Economic Impact of Cybercrime and Cyber Espionage*, July 2013, http://csis.org/files/publication/60396rpt_cybercrime-cost_0713_ph4_0.pdf.

[12] Ponemon Institute, *2013 Cost of Data Breach Study: Global Analysis*, 4-5, May 2013, https://www4.symantec.com/mktginfo/whitepaper/053013_GL_NA_WP_Ponemon-2013-Cost-of-a-Data-Breach-Report_daiNA_cta72382.pdf.

Data Protection and Security Laws

The prevalence, danger, and expense of attacks and unauthorized incursions into computer systems compel companies and people to put in place adequate security measures to protect their valuable and sensitive information. Because of the complexities of modern technology and networks, an army of information security professionals has arisen to protect the security of companies. Led by professionals with a systems and engineering background, these professionals, including Certified Information Systems Security Professionals (CISSP), seek to protect systems against mutating threats, including unauthorized access, compromised network security, and many other dangers.

Professionals with a technical background are not the only ones in an organization involved in security preparedness. Because a significant number of laws, regulations, and standards have grown up addressing the security of information, businesses should look beyond their engineering or IT staff to executives, general counsel, consultants, and outside legal counsel for assistance and guidance.

US Federal Laws

As previously discussed, many federal laws require businesses to maintain "reasonable" security, but do not mandate specific security measures. These laws include the HIPAA Security Rule, which requires covered entities to adopt measures to protect information and report data breaches of unsecured protected health information involving 500 or more individuals, the Graham-Leach-Bliley (GLB) Safeguards rule, which requires financial institutions to develop written information security plans, and COPPA, which mandates confidentiality, security and integrity of information in services targeting children. In addition, as will be discussed in Chapter 7, the FTC has authority under Section 5 of the FTC Act to exact penalties against entities misrepresenting their security protection measures.

Federal laws of broader scope also affect data security. The Sarbanes-Oxley Act of 2002 (SOX),[13] which increased the requirements for accurate

---

[13] Sarbanes-Oxley Act of 2002 [hereinafter SOX], Pub. L. No. 107-204, 1116 Stat. 745 (2002).

financial reporting for public companies and accounting firms in the wake of several financial accounting scandals, including that involving Enron, makes executives personally responsible for failing to oversee and establish a secure data environment.

Section 302[14] of SOX requires CEOs and CFOs to personally certify that financial reports are accurate and complete and Section 404[15] requires a corporation to assess the effectiveness of its internal controls and report this assessment annually to the SEC. The combined effect of these sections is that corporate officers must ensure that data security systems are in place and are effective. Although data security is not specifically mentioned in these sections or elsewhere in SOX, the reality is that "[a]ny review of internal controls would not be complete without addressing controls around information security. An insecure system would not be considered a source of reliable financial information because of the possibility of unauthorized transactions or manipulation of numbers."[16]

SOX requires an organization to "understand the nature of all transactions and corresponding data flows and implement appropriate controls to effectively prevent fraud, tampering, and manipulation of information."[17] A business and its corporate officers may be held responsible for poorly designed or operated systems, systems without sufficient internal controls, and for the failure to report breaches or unauthorized access to systems.[18] Because personal and proprietary information is often among the most important assets of a business, the requirements for protecting the integrity of such assets under SOX are important, not only because of the value of the data itself, but because of the potential for criminal and civil prosecution under the act.

The SEC has also promulgated rules for brokers, dealers, and investment companies under Regulation S-P (the Safeguards Rule), including the

---

[14] SOX § 302 codified at 15 U.S.C. § 7241 (West).

[15] SOX § 404 codified at 15 U.S.C. § 7262 (West).

[16] SANS Institute InfoSec Reading Room, *An Overview of Sarbanes-Oxley for the Information Security Professional*, 4, http://www.sans.org/reading-room/whitepapers/legal/overview-sarbanes-oxley-information-security-professional-1426?show=overview-sarbanes-oxley-information-security-professional-1426&cat=legal.

[17] INFORMATION SECURITY AND PRIVACY: A PRACTICAL GUIDE FOR GLOBAL EXECUTIVES, LAWYERS AND TECHNOLOGISTS 39 (Thomas J. Shaw, ed., 2011).

[18] *Id.* at 40.

obligation that these entities "adopt written policies and procedures that address administrative, technical, and physical safeguards for the protection of customer records and information."[19] The Safeguards Rule requires that an entity's policies and procedures must "(1) [i]nsure the security and confidentiality of customer records and information; (2) [p]rotect against any anticipated threats or hazards to the security or integrity of customer records and information; and (3) [p]rotect against unauthorized access to or use of customer records or information that could result in substantial harm or inconvenience to any customer."[20]

The SEC Division of Corporation Finance has also urged public companies to disclose security risks and cyber incidents under their broader disclosure obligations under the securities laws because such risks may be a significant factor in a decision to make an investment in a company "speculative or risky."[21] Despite this requirement, some companies do not disclose breaches because of ambiguity as to whether breaches are "material," the difficulty of quantifying losses from breaches, or for other reasons. The relative paucity of corporate breach disclosures has led some in Congress to call on the SEC to issue stronger guidelines for disclosing breaches and risks.[22]

US Executive Orders and Proposed Laws

On February 12, 2013, President Obama announced in his Fifth State of the Union Address that he had issued an Executive Order addressing cybersecurity for the country's critical infrastructure. The Executive Order, which was issued on the same day, requires a draft framework to be developed to allow the government to share intelligence on cyber-attacks with private critical infrastructure companies to allow them to better protect themselves. "Critical infrastructure" is defined broadly as "systems and assets, whether physical or virtual, so vital to the United States that the incapacity or destruction of such systems and assets would

---

[19] 17 C.F.R. § 248.30(a) (West).
[20] *Id.*
[21] Securities & Exchange Commission, *CF Disclosure Guidance: Topic 2 Cybersecurity*, Oct. 30, 2011, http://www.sec.gov/divisions/corpfin/guidance/ cfguidance-topic2.htm.
[22] Chris Strohm, *SEC Chairman Reviewing Company Cybersecurity Disclosures*, BLOOMBERG, May 13, 2013, http://www.bloomberg.com/news/2013-05-13/sec-chairman-reviewing-company-cybersecurity-disclosures.html.

have a debilitating impact on security, national economic security, national public health or safety, or any combination of those matters."[23]

The president has charged the National Institute of Standards and Technology (NIST), an agency of the Department of Commerce, with developing a cybersecurity framework for the critical infrastructure companies referenced in the Executive Order. The NIST in 2013 conducted workshops for stakeholders to help develop this voluntary framework and in late August 2013 submitted a discussion draft of the framework for review and comment.[24] The White House has also announced that it is considering incentives for cybersecurity preparedness for businesses, including cybersecurity insurance, grants, preferences for technical assistance and other processes, limitations on liability, streamlining regulation, public recognition of companies, rate recovery for price regulated industries, and cybersecurity research.[25]

Increased cybersecurity incursions and the losses they create have prompted many federal legislative proposals, but little enacted legislation. Among the more recent proposed laws is the Cyber Intelligence Sharing and Protection Act (CISPA). CISPA, which was passed by the House of Representatives on April 18, 2013, would require the US government and private companies to share Internet traffic information to prevent hackers from accessing valuable proprietary information, such as patents or trade secrets.[26]

The ACLU and other consumer groups oppose CISPA on the ground that it would "create a cybersecurity exception to all privacy laws and allow companies to share the private and personal data they hold on their

---

[23] White House Office of the Press Secretary, *Executive Order – Improving Critical Infrastructure Cybersecurity*, Feb. 12, 2013, http://m.whitehouse.gov/the-press-office/2013/02/12/executive-order-improving-critical-infrastructure-cybersecurity.

[24] National Institute of Standards & Technology, *Discussion Draft of the Preliminary Cybersecurity Framework*, Aug. 28, 2013, http://www.nist.gov/itl/upload/discussion-draft_preliminary-cybersecurity-framework-082813.pdf.

[25] Michael Daniel, *Incentives to Support Adoption of the Cybersecurity Framework*, White House Blog, Aug. 6, 2013, http://www.whitehouse.gov/blog/2013/08/06/incentives-support-adoption-cybersecurity-framework.

[26] Cyber Intelligence Sharing and Protection Act, H.R. 624, 113th Cong. (2013).

American customers with the government for cybersecurity purposes."[27]
The ACLU also argues that CISPA would allow private information to
be shared directly with government agencies, like the NSA, and would
permit companies to "hack back" when attacked.[28] Because of privacy
concerns, President Obama said that he would veto the version of CISPA
passed by the House.

A Senate Committee has also approved separate legislation titled the
Cybersecurity Act of 2013. This law codifies NIST's mandate under the
Executive Order to develop cybersecurity standards by making it an
ongoing responsibility of the agency and directs NIST to continue
coordinating a national cybersecurity awareness and preparedness
campaign without conferring any new regulatory authority on any federal
agency or department.[29]

Because of the controversies over the revelations about the NSA's
activities in collecting telephony metadata discussed in Chapter 9, it is
uncertain whether cybersecurity legislation will pass Congress in the
near future. Nonetheless, threats to critical infrastructure and businesses
persist, as well as the potentially catastrophic harms that may result from
malicious attacks.

US State Security Laws

The laws of several states require businesses to maintain the security of
information. California requires a "business that owns or licenses
personal information about a California resident [to] implement and
maintain reasonable security procedures and practices appropriate to the
nature of the information, to protect the personal information from
unauthorized access, destruction, use, modification or disclosure."[30]

---

[27] American Civil Liberties Union, *ACLU Opposition to H.R. 3523, the Cyber Intelligence
Sharing and Protection Act of 2011*, Dec. 1, 2011, http://www.aclu.org/technology-and-
liberty/aclu-opposition-hr-3523-cyber-intelligence-sharing-and-protection-act-2011.
[28] American Civil Liberties Union, Letter to House of Representatives Urging No vote on
CISPA, Apr. 15, 2013, *available at* http://www.aclu.org/files/assets/aclu_letter_to_congress_
urging_no_vote_on_h.r._624_cispa_-_4.15.13.pdf.
[29] Cybersecurity Act of 2013, S. 1353, 113th Cong. (2013-2014).
[30] Ann. Cal. Civil Code § 1798.81.5(b) (West).

Nevada has a similar law, but also requires data collectors to use encryption in transferring personal information outside a secure system or in moving a storage device containing personal information "beyond the logical or physical controls of the data collector" without using encryption.[31] Nevada law also provides that a data collector is not responsible for breaches of security if it is in compliance with these requirements.

US State Data Breach Notification Laws

The most common area for state legislation in the data security field is the requirement that organizations experiencing a data breach involving personal information notify affected consumers. As of July 1, 2013, forty-six states, the District of Columbia, Puerto Rico, and the Virgin Islands have such laws. Only Alabama, Kentucky, New Mexico and South Dakota remain outliers.

Although state laws differ, there are several common features to data breach notification laws that can be illustrated by the first of these laws from California. The California law[32] applies to persons or businesses that conduct business in California owning or licensing computerized data that includes personal information.

Businesses are required to "disclose any breach of the security of the system following discovery or notification of the breach in the security of the data to any resident of California whose unencrypted personal information was, or is reasonably believed to have been, acquired by an unauthorized person."[33] Personal information includes social security numbers, driver's license or California identification card numbers, account numbers in combination with required security or access codes or passwords, medical information, and health insurance information.[34] A "breach of the security of the system" is an "unauthorized acquisition of computerized data that compromises the security, confidentiality, or integrity of personal information maintained by the person or business."[35]

---

[31] Nev. Rev. Stat. Ann. § 603A.215 (West).
[32] *See* Ann. Cal. Civ. Code § 1798.82 (West).
[33] Ann. Cal. Civ. Code § 1798.82(a).
[34] Ann. Cal. Civ. Code § 1798.82(h).
[35] Ann. Cal. Civ. Code § 1798.82(g).

An amendment to the law, which will go into effect on January 1, 2014, expands the definition of personal information requiring notification of a breach to include "[a] user name or email address, in combination with a password or security question and answer that would permit access to an online account."[36] The amendment was designed to address the situation of hackers accessing unencrypted passwords, as publicized in recent breaches of social networking sites.

California's law further requires that notice must be given "in the most expedient time possible and without unreasonable delay, consistent with the legitimate needs of law enforcement...or any measures necessary to determine the scope of the breach and restore the reasonable integrity of the data system."[37] If a single breach involves more than 500 California residents, a copy of the notice must also be sent to the California attorney general.[38] The law also requires that the notification be written or electronic and be written "in plain language" and include, at a minimum:

- Name and contact information of the reporting person or business;
- Types of personal information subject to the breach;
- Date or estimated date or date range of the breach;
- Whether the breach was delayed because of law enforcement investigation;
- General description of the breach incident; and
- Toll-free numbers and addresses of the major credit reporting agencies, if social security numbers or identification numbers were involved in the breach.[39]

If an entity experiencing a breach does not own the information (as where a third party processes information owned by others), it must notify the owner of the breach.[40] Waivers of the California breach notification law are contrary to public policy and are void and unenforceable. There is also a private right of action to enforce the law.[41]

---

[36] Senate Bill No. 46 (C.A.) (adding Cal. Civil Code § 1798.82(h)(2)).

[37] Ann. Cal. Civ. Code § 1798.82(a).

[38] Ann. Cal. Civ. Code § 1798.82(f).

[39] Ann. Cal. Civ. Code § 1798.82(d).

[40] Ann. Cal. Civ. Code § 1798.82(b).

[41] Ann. Cal. Civ. Code § 1798.84(a)-(b).

California's data breach notification law does not require any threshold for harm to affected individuals to trigger the notification obligation. A subject of a data breach of unencrypted information is thus required to report data breaches that may have little or no chance of harming California residents through identity theft or otherwise.

In contrast, Ohio, Pennsylvania, and some other states only require notice if there is a determination or reasonable belief that the breach of personal information will cause harm to the affected individuals. Ohio, for example, requires notification only for a "breach of the security of the system" that "causes, reasonably is believed to have caused, or reasonably is believed will cause a material risk of identity theft or other fraud to the person or property of a resident of this state."[42]

State data breach notification laws differ in their definitions of personal information, which may include biometric data, unique electronic identifiers, taxpayer identification numbers, fingerprints, DNA profiles, computer passwords, mother's maiden name, or birth or marriage certificate numbers.[43] State laws also vary as to whether breach notification is required for paper records, the notification procedures to be followed, whether specific content is required in the notice, and whether notice must be made to state officials, such as the attorney general.[44]

The 2012 California attorney general's report about data breaches provides some insight into the extent of data breaches in the state. The report found that 2.5 million people in the state were affected by 131 data breaches involving more than 500 Californians in 2012. The report concluded that "[m]ore than 1.4 million Californians would not have been put at risk and 28 percent of the data breaches would not have required notification, if the data had been encrypted."

The California attorney general recommended that companies encrypt digital personal information when moving or sending it out of their

---

[42] Ohio Rev. Code § 1349.19(A)(1)(a) (West 2007).
[43] For a useful outline of state breach notification laws *see* Mintz Levin, *State Data Security Breach Notification Laws*, Jul. 15, 2013, http://www.mintz.com/newsletter/ 2007/PrivSec-DataBreachLaws-02-07/state_data_breach_matrix.pdf.
[44] *Id.*

secure network; that they review and tighten security controls on personal information, including training employees and customers; improve the readability of breach notices; offer mitigation products or provide information on security freezes to victims involving breaches of social security numbers or driver's license numbers; and that California's breach notification law be amended to require notification of breaches of online credentials, such as user name and password.[45] As noted, such a change will in fact come into effect in California on January 1, 2014.

Self-Governing and Other Security Standards

In addition to legal mandates, contracts may impose requirements on businesses for securing personal information. For example, the Payment Card Industry Data Security Standards (PCI DSS) promulgated by the payment card industry mandate security standards for businesses worldwide accepting credit cards. The PCI DSS require businesses to follow specific security standards when cardholder data, including account numbers and names and sensitive authentication data (such as the information contained on a magnetic strip), is stored, processed, or transmitted.[46]

The PCI DSS includes principles for building and maintaining a secure network, protecting cardholder data, maintaining a vulnerability management program, putting in place strong access control measures, regularly monitoring and testing networks, and maintaining an information security network.[47] The PCI DSS also contain many other specific requirements, including maintaining firewalls, prohibiting public Internet access to the cardholder data environment, encrypting data, minimizing cardholder data storage, and forbidding storage of sensitive authentication data.[48]

Although the PCI DSS generally do not have the force of law, they may establish a standard for determining whether a company's security

---

[45] California Attorney General, *Data Breach Report 2012*, at iii-iv, http://oag.ca.gov/sites/all/files/agweb/pdfs/privacy/2012data_breach_rpt.pdf.
[46] *See* Payment Card Industry (PCI) Data Security Standard, *Navigating PCI DSS v. 2.0*, Oct. 2010, https://www.pcisecuritystandards.org/documents/navigating_dss_v20.pdf.
[47] *Id.* at 10.
[48] *Id.* at 14, 20-21.

practices are "reasonable" under legal requirements. If a company violates the standards, it may be subject to penalties by acquiring banks and have its relationship with the banks terminated (and thus be unable to process credit cards).[49] Several states, including Minnesota, Nevada, and Oregon, also require some businesses to comply with PCI DSS.[50]

Both government and non-government standard organizations have promulgated other frequently used security standards. The NIST has issued many standards, including its Security and Privacy Controls for Federal Information Systems and Organizations (NIST Special Publication 800-53) now in its fourth revision.[51] This publication provides a "catalog of security and privacy controls...to protect organizational operations (including mission, functions, image and reputation), organizational assets, individuals, other organizations, and the Nation from a diverse set of threats including hostile cyber attacks, natural disasters, structural failure, and human errors (both intentional and unintentional)."[52]

The International Organization for Standardization (IOS) and the International Electrotechnical Commission (IEC) have also published information technology security techniques standards with global application for management systems and information security management (ISO 27001:2005 and ISO 27002). The objective of ISO 27001 is to "provide a model for establishing, implementing, operating, monitoring, reviewing, maintaining, and improving an Information Security Management System" appropriate for the "size and structure of the organization."[53]

ISO 27002 is a "code of practice for information security" that "outlines hundreds of potential controls and control mechanisms, which may be

---

[49] PCI Compliance Guide, *PCI FAQs and Myths*, http://www.pcicomplianceguide.org/pcifaqs. php.

[50] Minn. Stat. § 325E.64 (West 2007); Nev. Rev. Stat. § 603A.215 (West); Wash. Rev. Code § 19.255.020 (West).

[51] NIST Special Publication 800-53 Revision 4, *Security and Privacy Controls for Federal Information Systems and Organizations*, April 2013, http://nvlpubs.nist.gov/nistpubs/Special Publications/NIST.SP.800-53r4.pdf.

[52] *Id.* at iii.

[53] The ISO 27000 Directory, *An Introduction to ISO 27001*, http://www.27000.org/iso-27001.htm. A new draft ISO 27001:2013 was released in 2013. http://www.iso-27001-it-security-management.com/what-iso27001-certification.htm.

implemented, in theory, subject to the guidance provided within ISO 27001."[54] Many organizations seek to have an "information security management system" (ISMS) certified as ISO 27001 compliant by an accredited registrar.

Liability for Data Breaches

Other chapters in this book outline potential sources of liability for entities experiencing a data breach involving personal information, including regulatory actions by the Office for Civil Rights of the Department of Health and Human Services for violation of the HIPAA Security Rule, FTC enforcement of the GLB Safeguards Rule and Section 5 of the FTC Act, and private lawsuits under state laws, such as the California Medical Information Act.

Companies and their officers and directors may also be responsible for breaches under other laws. In 2008, for example, the SEC levied a $275,000 penalty on a financial services firm experiencing multiple hacking incidents for its failure to have a written data security policy and to take security measures in response to identified weaknesses.[55] Using its authority under the Safeguards Rule, the SEC penalized the firm for not carrying out timely corrective actions that would have prevented security breaches.

Another potential source for liability for inadequate data security is a shareholder derivative lawsuit brought by shareholders of the corporation alleging that the corporation failed to follow corporate law. A typical shareholder derivative action alleges that members of the board of directors breached their fiduciary duties by failing to ensure that a "corporate information and reporting system, which the board concludes is adequate, exists..."[56] Lawsuits of this type are often based on the failure of a board to take action, rather than having taken inadequate

---

[54] The ISO 27000 Directory, *Introduction to ISO 27002*, http://www.27000.org/iso-27002.htm.

[55] Press Release, Securities and Exchange Commission, *SEC Charges LPL Financial for Failing to Protect Customer Privacy*, Sept. 11, 2008, http://www.sec.gov/news/press/2008/2008-193.htm.

[56] *In re Caremark Int'l Inc. Derivative Litig.*, 698 A.2d 959, 970 (Del.Ch. 1996).

action. Although many corporations mount effective defenses to such lawsuits, shareholder derivative suits are expensive, generate negative publicity, and substantially divert executive and board resources.[57]

An example of a shareholder lawsuit is the 2010 Delaware Chancery Court action by shareholders of TJX Companies Inc., which operates TJ Maxx retail stores, against the company's board of directors. The shareholders alleged that the board breached its fiduciary duty by allowing hackers from 2005 to 2007 to gain access to credit card information stored in the company's computer system. The lawsuit further alleged that these attacks caused damage to the company, including settlements with credit card companies and the costs of defending a class action, notifying customers, and conducting forensic investigations.[58] The company settled the lawsuit for an undisclosed amount in 2010.

Besides derivative actions, shareholders may bring direct actions against companies under the Securities Exchange Act of 1934 alleging that data breaches have decreased the share price of the company's stock. An example of such a lawsuit is *In re Choicepoint, Inc. Securities Litigation*, in which shareholders alleged that a data broker hid information about hacking that, when made public, led to a significant drop in share value. The company later paid $10 million to settle the lawsuit.[59]

State attorneys general may also pursue actions against companies for security breaches under the authority of the states' data breach notification laws. The Indiana attorney general, for example, sued a health insurer when it made disclosures of personal information of customers on the Internet. The lawsuit settled for a $100,000 payment to the state.[60]

---

[57] Steven L. Capponi, *Cybersecurity and the Board of Directors: Avoiding Personal Liability* (July 25, 2013), Thomas Reuters Accelus, http://www.blankrome.com/index.cfm?contentID=37&itemID=3145.
[58] *Louisiana Mun. Police Employees' Ret. Sys. v. Alvarez*, 2010 WL 2735670 (Del. Ch. July 2, 2010) (Stipulation and Agreement of Settlement of Derivative Litigation).
[59] Jaikumar Vijayan, *ChoicePoint to Pay $10M to Settle Last Breach-Related Lawsuit*, Jan. 28, 2008, COMPUTERWORLD http://www.computerworld.com/s/article/9059659/ChoicePoint_to_pay_10M_to_settle_last_breach_related_lawsuit.
[60] Press Release, Indiana Attorney General, *Attorney General Reaches Settlement with WellPoint in Consumer Data Breach*, Jul. 5, 2011, http://www.in.gov/portal/news_events/71252.htm.

7

The Federal Trade Commission as Privacy and Data Security Enforcer

The Federal Trade Commission (FTC) was established in 1914 under the Federal Trade Commission Act (FTC Act) as an independent commission of the US government. Although the FTC has important functions in enforcing antitrust laws and requirements relating to mergers, it is also the most prominent federal consumer protection agency. Besides its powers relating to advertising, marketing, credit and finance, the FTC has emerged as the nation's privacy and data security watchdog. Then Chairman Jon Leibowitz referred to the FTC in 2012 as the "nation's privacy protection agency."[1]

The FTC has authority to enforce thirty-three federal privacy provisions, including COPPA, FCRA, GLB, the Red Flags Rule, and the US-EU Safe Harbor Framework. Besides its specific authority under these laws, the FTC has power to enforce privacy and data security matters under Section 5 of the FTC Act.[2]

Although Section 5 dates back to 1914, the FTC's use of its powers for privacy and data security matters arose in the Internet age. From about 1995, the FTC has focused on the consumer implications of the Internet.

In 1998 the FTC prepared a report on online privacy to Congress highlighting that the Internet is not only a great boon for consumers, but

---

[1] Federal Trade Commission, *Press Remarks of Chairman Jon Leibowitz as Prepared for Delivery Release of Final FTC Privacy Report*, Mar. 26, 2012, http://www.ftc.gov/os/2012/03/120326jdlprivacyrptremarks.pdf.
[2] 15 U.S.C. § 45 (2006).

also a source of concern because of its massive collection of personal information.[3] The FTC found that 92 percent of Internet sites collected information from consumers, but only 14 percent provided notice about information practices, and only 2 percent had a comprehensive privacy policy. The FTC therefore urged that the "widely accepted" FIPPs be applied to the Internet, including notice, choice, access, and security. The report also stressed the problems surrounding collection of information from children online and called for legislation in this area, which was enacted as COPPA later in 1998.[4]

The FTC again cited the FIPPs in a May 2000 Report to Congress on *Privacy Online: Fair Information Practices in the Electronic Marketplace.*[5] Although only two years had passed since its prior report, the FTC stressed that the "online consumer marketplace is growing at an exponential rate" and "technology has enhanced the capacity of online companies to collect, store, transfer, and analyze vast amounts of data from and about the consumers who visit their Web sites."[6] The FTC proposed that Congress enact legislation to require consumer-oriented Internet sites to follow the "four widely-accepted fair information principles" of notice, choice, access, and security.[7]

Unlike its 1998 report, which stimulated the enactment of COPPA, the FTC's 2000 report did not result in Congressional action. Nonetheless, the FTC has continued to lobby for legislation based on the FIPPs. Most recently, the FTC in 2012 issued a report on *Protecting Consumer Privacy in an Era of Rapid Change: Recommendations for Businesses and Policymakers* that makes several new consumer protection proposals.[8] The FTC proposed in the report a "privacy framework" that is "intended to assist Congress as it considers privacy legislation." The framework consists of

---

[3] Federal Trade Commission, *Privacy Online: A Report to Congress*, 23, 27, 29, Jun. 1998, [hereinafter FTC 1998 Report], http://www.ftc.gov/reports/privacy3/priv-23a.pdf.
[4] *Id.*

[5] Federal Trade Commission, *Privacy Online: Fair Information Practices in the Electronic Marketplace: A Report to Congress*, May 2000, http://www.ftc.gov/reports/privacy2000/privacy2000.pdf.
[6] *Id.*

[7] *Id.* at i-iii.

[8] Federal Trade Commission, *Protecting Consumer Privacy in an Era of Rapid Change*, 2012, http://ftc.gov/os/2012/03/120326privacyreport.pdf.

privacy by design, simplified consumer choice, and transparency. The framework also includes five major FTC action items:

1) A "do not track" (DNT) mechanism by which consumers can signal that they do not want to be tracked on the Internet;
2) Development of "short, meaningful [privacy] disclosures" for mobile services;
3) Legislation to provide consumers with access to information held about them by a data broker;
4) A focus on the "heightened privacy concerns" raised by large platforms, such as Internet service providers (ISPs), operating systems, browsers, and social media; and
5) Promotion of enforceable self-regulatory and sector-specific codes of conduct, in conjunction with the Department of Commerce.[9]

Despite its lack of success in having privacy legislation enacted at the federal level, the FTC has emerged since 2000 as the government's primary privacy enforcer through its use of Section 5 of the FTC Act. Under this authority, the FTC had brought many regulatory actions against organizations violating consumers' privacy rights or failing to maintain the security of personal information.

Section 5 declares unlawful "[u]nfair methods of competition in or affecting commerce, and unfair or deceptive acts or practices in or affecting commerce" and gives the FTC the power to investigate such acts or practices and to prevent businesses, except for financial organizations, from engaging in such practices. The FTC's authority under Section 5 thus has two separate bases—unfairness and deception.

Under the "unfairness" prong, the FTC focuses on consumer injury as a result of unfair practices. As interpreted by the FTC, an act or practice is unfair if it "[c]auses or is likely to cause substantial injury to consumers; [c]annot be reasonably avoided by consumers, and [i]s not outweighed by countervailing benefits to consumers or to competition."[10] The unfairness prong requires at least a likelihood of "substantial injury" or consumer harm.

---

[9] *Id.* at v-vi.

[10] Federal Reserve Board, *Federal Reserve Board Consumer Compliance Handbook, Federal Trade Commission Act Section 5: Unfair or Deceptive Acts or Practices* (June 2008), http://www.federalreserve.gov/boarddocs/supmanual/cch/ftca.pdf.

Deceptive acts or practices are those where "[a] representation, omission, or practice misleads or is likely to mislead the consumer; [a] consumer's interpretation of the representation, omission, or practice is considered reasonable under the circumstances; and [t]he misleading representation, omission, or practice is material."[11] Under the deception prong, actual deception need not be shown, nor is it necessary to show that a company intended to defraud or deceive consumers.

Although Section 5 gives the FTC powers to investigate and, under certain circumstances, to levy civil penalties against companies, there is no private right of action under the FTC Act nor is there an opportunity for interested third parties to become involved in such investigations. There is also no judicial review of FTC regulatory analyses.[12]

The FTC frequently proceeds through negotiating consent decrees with companies that it accuses of engaging in unfair or deceptive practices. Once final, violations of consent orders, by which a company voluntarily agrees to cease its objectionable conduct without admitting it has violated the law, may be enforced with civil penalties. If a settlement cannot be reached, the FTC may bring an enforcement action under Section 5 through a complaint heard by an administrative law judge. Final FTC decisions, which consist of cease and desist orders, may be appealed to a US Court of Appeal.[13] The FTC may also bring civil actions in court for violations of "unfair or deceptive acts or practices."[14]

Since 1997, the FTC has lodged over 150 privacy complaints against businesses under Section 5. The number of these complaints has increased over the years, with nineteen complaints being brought in 2012 alone. The body of these complaints and the resulting consent decrees creates a unique body of privacy law some say is akin to a body of common law.[15]

---

[11] *Id.*

[12] 15 U.S.C. § 57b-3 (West).

[13] Electronic Privacy information Center, *Federal Trade Commission Overview of Statutory Authority to Remedy Privacy Infringements, available at* http://epic.org/privacy/internet/ftc/Authority.html#fn3.

[14] *See* 15 U.S.C. § 57b (West).

[15] Daniel J. Solove & Woodrow Hartzog, *The FTC and the New Common Law of Privacy,* 114 COLUMBIA LAW REV. (forthcoming 2014) at 11. Tthis view has been disputed. *See* Alan Friel, *Why We Don't Need the FTC on Big Data Lifeguard Duty,* ADVERTISING AGE, Oct. 8, 2013,

Recent FTC Enforcement Actions

Recent FTC enforcement actions for privacy and security matters illustrate the wide range of the FTC's authority under Section 5.

Google

FTC fined Google $22.5 million in 2012 for allegedly engaging in misrepresentations concerning Apple's Safari browser and for violating a prior consent order.[16] Google's settlement of the 2012 Safari case is the largest FTC penalty ever for violating an order of the commission.

Google, which operates the most popular Internet search engine, earns billions of dollars of revenue in delivering targeted ads to consumers online. Google obtains information about users from "cookies" placed on a user's computer that can be accessed to target advertisements to consumers. For example, a person doing a Google search for a hotel in San Diego may find that she is presented with advertisements for a specific San Diego hotel when browsing on a non-Google website.

The gist of the FTC's complaint is that Google placed advertising cookies on the computers of Safari users, even though Google had previously told users that they would be automatically opted out of tracking as a result of the browser's default settings. The FTC also charged that Google circumvented the browser's default settings by placing a temporary cookie on the browser opening the door to other Google cookies.

The FTC alleged that Google's actions violated a prior settlement with the FTC that barred Google from misrepresenting the extent to which consumers can exercise control over their information. In the 2011 case, the FTC alleged that Google used misleading tactics in its "Buzz"

---

available at http://adage.com/article/privacy-and-regulation/ftc-big-data-lifeguard-duty/244128/, (arguing that FTC's unfairness actions "in the absence of definitive laws or rules is disruptive to industry and implicates issues of notice and due process, or rather the lack thereof").

[16] Press Release, Federal Trade Commission, *Google Will Pay $22.5 Million to Settle FTC Charges it Misrepresented Privacy Assurances to Users of Apple's Safari Internet Browser* (Aug. 9, 2012), *available at* http://ftc.gov/opa/2012/08/google.shtm.

social network, including leading Gmail users to believe they could choose not to join Buzz, when in fact that option was ineffective.[17] In settling the Buzz matter, Google agreed to carry out a comprehensive privacy program to protect consumer data. As the FTC said in the press release announcing the settlement, this was "the first time an FTC settlement order has required a company to implement a comprehensive privacy program to protect the privacy of consumers' information." In another first, the FTC settled claims that Google violated the US-EU Safe Harbor Framework.[18]

Myspace

The FTC in 2012 reached a privacy settlement with Myspace—a social networking pioneer—for having misrepresented the privacy protections it gives users' personal information. In announcing the settlement, the FTC said that it was one of several cases that the commission had brought in its "ongoing efforts [to] make sure companies live up to the privacy promises they make to consumers."[19]

Although Myspace promised in its privacy policy that it would not provide personally identifiable information to third parties without first giving notice to users and receiving their permission, it was alleged to have given that information to advertisers when users browsed pages on the site. The FTC further charged that advertisers could locate users' Myspace profiles to get more information about the user, including the user's full name. Advertisers could then combine the user's real name and other personal information to link web browsing to a specific person.

The settlement barred Myspace from misrepresenting the extent to which it protects the privacy of users' information. Myspace settled the charge that it had engaged in deceptive practices by agreeing to establish a

---

[17] Press Release, Federal Trade Commission, *FTC Charges Deceptive Privacy Practices in Google's Rollout of Its Buzz Social Network* (Mar. 20, 2011), *available at* http://www.ftc.gov/opa/2011/03/google.shtm.

[18] *Id.*

[19] Press Release, Federal Trade Commission, *Myspace Settles FTC Charges That It Misled Millions of Users About Sharing Personal Information with Advertisers* (May 8, 2012), *available at* http://www.ftc.gov/opa/2012/05/myspace.shtm.

comprehensive privacy program protecting consumers' information and by undertaking twenty years of biennial privacy assessments by independent, third-party auditors.[20]

Wyndham Hotels

Besides enforcing the privacy promises companies make, the FTC has brought actions against businesses for security failures leading to data breaches. In a recent case, the FTC filed a lawsuit against Wyndham Worldwide Corporation for security failures for data breaches of personal information, including payment card information sent to a domain address in Russia.[21] The FTC alleged that, despite Wyndham Hotels' statement that it protected personal privacy, the company "failed to take security measures such as complex user IDs and passwords, firewalls and network segmentation between the hotels and the corporate network."[22]

The case is unusual because Wyndham, unlike other companies, has challenged the right of the FTC under Section 5 to bring actions for an entity's failure to protect consumers' personal data. In a motion to dismiss the case, Wyndham claimed that the FTC is impermissibly intruding into the area of data security standards for the private sector that is the domain of Congress and about which Congress has failed to act. The FTC responded by noting that it has brought forty-one actions against companies alleging breaches of data security standards and that its authority under Section 5 must be sufficiently broad to meet the ongoing consumer protection challenges in the Internet age.

Facebook

The FTC in 2012 approved a settlement with Facebook concerning its charge that the social networking company had deceived consumers by representing that it kept users' information private, when in fact it made

---

[20] *Id.*

[21] Press Release, Federal Trade Commission, *FTC Files Complaint Against Wyndham Hotels for Failure to Protect Consumers' Personal Information* (Jun. 26, 2012), *available at* http://www.ftc.gov/opa/2012/06/wyndham.shtm.

[22] *Id.*

information public.[23] The FTC charged that Facebook's privacy pages did not disclose that a user's choice to restrict information to "only friends" or "friends of friends" would be ineffective as to third parties and that this information could be accessed by applications used by friends.

Facebook's settlement with the FTC requires Facebook to take future measures "to make sure it lives up to its promises...including by giving consumers clear and prominent notice and obtaining their express consent before sharing their information beyond their privacy settings, by maintaining a comprehensive privacy program to protect consumers' information, and by obtaining biennial privacy audits from an independent third party."[24]

Twitter

The FTC in 2010 settled charges with Twitter that it put consumers' privacy at risk by not safeguarding personal information. Although Twitter had a privacy policy in which it said that it employed "administrative, physical and electronic measures designed to protect [consumers'] information from unauthorized access," hackers were able to gain administrative control of the service.[25] The FTC charged that hackers were able to do this by using a password-guessing tool because Twitter had set the administrative password as a weak, lowercase, common dictionary word. Hackers used their access to send phony tweets from various accounts, including from then President-elect Obama and Fox News.

The FTC alleged that Twitter was vulnerable to attack because it did not require hard-to-guess administrative passwords, enforce password changes, restrict administrative access controls to employees whose jobs required them, and impose other reasonable restrictions, such as only allowing access from specific IP addresses.

---

[23] Press Release, Federal Trade Commission, *FTC Approves Final Settlement with Facebook* (Aug. 10, 2012), *available at* http://www.ftc.gov/opa/2012/08/facebook.shtm.
[24] *Id.*
[25] Press Release, Federal Trade Commission, *Twitter Settles Charges that it Failed to Protect Consumers' Personal Information; Company Will Establish Independently Audited Information Security Program* (June 24, 2010), *available at* http://www.ftc.gov/opa/2010/06/twitter.shtm.

Under the settlement, Twitter was barred for twenty years from misleading consumers about the extent it protected privacy and security and had to establish and maintain a comprehensive information security program assessed by an independent auditor.

8

Privacy Litigation

Because of the litigiousness of United States society, the availability of contingency fee arrangements, class actions that can garner massive damage awards, settlements and attorney fees, and the publicity given to alleged privacy violations of prominent companies, privacy litigation is an established phenomenon. Although privacy litigation is not new, it has taken on different colors in the Internet era. A typical invasion of privacy case in the past might have involved publication of a news story about a recluse or a photograph to which the subject had not given consent.[1] Privacy litigation today, in contrast, is often directed to technology or Internet companies alleged to have shared information without users' consent or in violation of a privacy policy.

Lawsuits based on invasion of privacy rights have always faced legal challenges. In the past, defendants in invasion of privacy lawsuits often claimed that the press had the right to publish information about the plaintiffs under the First Amendment. A defendant today is more likely to attack the plaintiff's lack of "standing" or damages than to defend on freedom of speech grounds. The shift reflects the reality that current privacy lawsuits are based on commercial conduct—not dissemination of information to the press. Although relatively few privacy lawsuits involving personal data go to trial, the potential challenges posed by such lawsuits are an established part of the privacy law ecosystem in this country.

---

[1] *See, e.g., Dietemann v. Time, Inc.*, 449 F.2d 245 (9th Cir. 1971) (*Life* magazine surreptitiously photographed the plaintiff for a story exposing "quackery").

Recent Privacy Litigation Cases

Most prominent technology and Internet companies have been sued for alleged privacy violations in recent years because of the attention paid to their privacy practices and the large number of affected consumers. Although companies of any size can be sued, recent cases against AOL, Facebook, Apple, and Google illustrate the challenges and potential risks of privacy lawsuits.

AOL

AOL in 2006 posted a database of confidential web searches of over 650,000 users on the Internet for research purposes. Although the posted information did not contain user names and was supposedly "anonymized," it was possible for journalists at the *New York Times* to identify AOL subscribers from the information.[2] After these revelations, plaintiffs sued AOL under the Wiretap Act, the California Consumer Legal Remedies Act, California false advertising law, and California unfair competition laws for revealing their personal information.[3]

In what has become an expected step in privacy litigation, AOL moved to dismiss the case because plaintiffs had not established "standing" under Article III of the US Constitution. AOL also argued that plaintiffs had not sufficiently alleged injury and causation of their claims or stated a proper claim that it had violated any law.

"Standing" is a legal concept addressed at the beginning of a lawsuit to determine whether the plaintiff has a sufficient stake in the matter for a court to hear the dispute. The doctrine of standing has developed to ensure that only disputes appropriately resolved through the judicial process (as opposed to those best determined by the legislative or executive branches) remain in the court system. Although standing is a technical legal question, non-lawyers may be familiar with the concept because of the Supreme

---

[2] Michael Barbaro & Tom Zeller, Jr., *A Face is Exposed for AOL Searcher No. 4417749*, N.Y. TIMES, Aug. 9, 2006, *available at* http://www.nytimes.com/2006/08/09/technology/09aol. html?_r=0.

[3] *Doe 1 v. AOL LLC*, 719 F. Supp. 2d 1102, 1105 (N.D. Cal. 2010).

Court's recent decision that the proponents of California's Proposition 8 prohibiting gay marriage did not have standing to oppose a lower court decision that the law violated the US Constitution. Because the jurisdiction of US federal courts is based on Article III of the Constitution, standing in those courts is referred to as "Article III standing." [4]

Article III standing requires generally that a plaintiff allege "injury in fact"—an injury that is "actual or imminent, not 'conjectural' or 'hypothetical.'" [5] Standing also requires that there be a causal connection between the injury and the conduct complained of and that it be "'likely,' as opposed to merely 'speculative,' that the injury will be 'redressed by a favorable decision' [by the court]." [6] In the *AOL* case, the court concluded that the plaintiffs indeed did have standing to bring their claims.

In addition to standing, plaintiffs bringing claims in a lawsuit normally must allege injury or damages under a specific law. In the *AOL* lawsuit, defendants sought to dismiss plaintiffs' claims because they had not claimed damages under any law. The court disagreed because AOL had "held itself out to the market as being a leader in internet security and privacy and represented that it assured members that its service was 'safe, secure and private.'" The court also ruled that AOL's disclosure of "members' undeniably sensitive information is not something that members bargained for when they signed up and paid fees for AOL's service." [7]

The *AOL* case shows the costs that privacy litigation can exact on a company. After almost seven years of expensive litigation, a judge gave final approval to a class action settlement between plaintiffs and AOL on May 24, 2013. The settlement required the payment of $5 million to class members and nearly $1 million in legal fees to class plaintiffs. As part of the settlement, AOL also had to maintain policies and procedures to prevent such incidents from happening in the future. [8]

---

[4] *Id.* at 1108-9.

[5] *See Lujan v. Defenders of Wildlife*, 504 U.S. 555, 560 (1992) (quoting *Whitmore v. Arkansas*, 495 U.S. 149, 155 (1990)).

[6] *See Lujan*, 504 U.S. at 560-1(quoting *Simon v. E. Kentucky Welfare Rights Org.*, 426 U.S. 26, 41-2, (1976))

[7] *See Doe 1*, 719 F. Supp. 2d at 1111-12.

[8] Paul Bond & Frederick Lah, *Court Grants Final Approval to Class Action Settlement Over AOL's 2006 Anonymization Failure; Big Data Precursor Settles for Millions*, Reed Smith Global Regulatory Enforcement Law Blog, May 30, 2013, http://www.globalregulatoryenforce

Facebook

Plaintiffs have frequently targeted Facebook in privacy litigation because of changes to its privacy policies and the ways in which it shares users' personal information. Two recent Facebook cases illustrate the range of litigation issues for social networking sites, which depend upon the personal information provided by users in return for free access to the sites. The cases also show the difficulties plaintiffs have in demonstrating harm from perceived privacy violations.

Plaintiffs alleged in 2010 that Facebook shared users' names, genders, pictures, and webpage addresses through transmission of a "referrer header" to third party advertisers without users' knowledge or consent, in violation of Facebook's own policies.[9] Plaintiffs brought claims under the Wiretap Act, the Stored Communications Act (SCA), and for violation of California state laws. Facebook moved to dismiss the claims on the grounds of lack of Article III standing and for failure to state proper claims under federal and state law.

The court concluded that plaintiffs had sufficiently alleged violations of their rights under the Wiretap Act and SCA to establish standing, but found that plaintiffs nonetheless could not bring those claims. The court reasoned that the Wiretap Act was not violated because Facebook was authorized to receive the communications containing personal information initiated by users. In a Catch-22 for plaintiffs, the court also held that if the communications were considered to be directed by users *to advertisers*, then the advertisers were the intended recipients of the message and the Wiretap Act again did not apply.[10] After giving the plaintiffs an opportunity to remedy these defects, the court permanently dismissed the lawsuit.[11]

Plaintiffs also sued Facebook in 2010 for its use of its "Friend Finder" feature which allows it to access e-mail accounts that a user has on other

---

mentlawblog.com/2013/05/articles/data-security/court-grants-final-approval-to-class-action-settlement-over-aols-2006-anonymization-failure-big-data-precursor-settles-for-millions/.

[9] *In re Facebook Privacy Litig.*, 791 F. Supp. 2d 705, 709 (N.D. Cal. 2011).

[10] *Id.*, 791 F. Supp.2d at 713.

[11] *See In re Facebook Privacy Litigation*, C 10-02389 JW, 2011 WL 6176208 (N.D. Cal. Nov. 22, 2011) (Order Granting Defendant's Motion to Dismiss with Prejudice).

services to suggest other Facebook members that a user can "friend." Plaintiffs complained that Friend Finder placed notifications on users' home pages stating that their Facebook friends had used the service when they had not authorized the use of their names and profile pictures for this purpose. They also alleged that Facebook had misappropriated users' names and likenesses, violated their trademark rights, and that the company had engaged in unfair competition.[12]

The court threw out the misappropriation and unfair competition claims because plaintiffs had not shown that they were injured by Facebook's conduct. As the court said, "[p]laintiffs have not shown how the mere disclosure to their Facebook friends that they have employed the Friend Finder service (even assuming some of them did not) causes them any cognizable harm, regardless of the extent to which that disclosure could have been seen as an implied endorsement by them of the service."[13]

The court also found that plaintiffs, who were non-celebrities, did not have a protectable economic interest in their identities sufficient to bring a trademark claim. After the plaintiffs filed an amended lawsuit alleging that their names and likenesses had value to Facebook, the court dismissed the case permanently for failure to allege damages. The court denied Facebook's effort to receive $706,000 for its lawyers' fees in defending the case.[14]

Apple

Plaintiffs owning iPhones and iPads brought a class action in 2011 against Apple and other companies alleging that Apple had impermissibly sent users' personal information, including the unique device identifier (UDID) associated with their devices, to third-party applications (apps) sold through Apple's store using its "iOS" operating system. Although users admitted that they had not been charged for the apps, they claimed that they had suffered monetary harm because Apple designed its devices to

---

[12] See Cohen v. Facebook, Inc., 798 F. Supp.2d 1090 (N.D. Cal. 2011).

[13] Cohen, 798 F. Supp.2d at 1097.

[14] Wendy Davis, Facebook, Consumers Settle 'Friend Finder' Dispute, ONLINE MEDIA DAILY, Sept. 14, 2012, http://www.mediapost.com/publications/article/182974/facebook-consumers-settle-friend-finder-dispute.html#axzz2f5JUgIpA.

allow personal information to be disclosed to third parties, including address, GPS information, unique device identifiers for the devices, gender, age, ZIP code, and time zone information.

Plaintiffs also claimed they were harmed because the applications consumed limited resources on their Apple devices including bandwidth and storage space. Plaintiffs alleged that information sent to the apps was not encrypted and that they had overpaid for their devices. Plaintiffs brought their claims under the Stored Communications Act, the Wiretap Act, the privacy provision of the California Constitution, the Computer Fraud and Abuse Act, and under various common law and California state law theories.[15]

The court rejected defendants' challenge to plaintiffs' Article III standing, finding that plaintiffs had sufficiently claimed that they had been injured and that the injuries could be traced to Apple. The court also concluded that plaintiffs went beyond the "theoretical allegations that personal information has independent economic value" by claiming that they had been harmed by diminished device resources, increased security risk, and their reliance on Apple's representations that it would protect their privacy.[16]

Despite its conclusion that plaintiffs had standing, the court rejected most of plaintiffs' claims. The court concluded that a person's iPhone or iPad is not a "facility through which an electronic communication service is provided" under the SCA because that would make the apps downloaded by plaintiffs "users" of a person's iPhone or iPad, which is an illogical result. The court also determined that defendants did not access data in "electronic storage" on plaintiffs' devices. The court ruled that Apple's actions fell within the law's exceptions for service providers or the intended recipients of communications and that Apple had not accessed a communications facility to obtain access to an electronic communication when it was in storage.[17]

---

[15] *In re iPhone Application Litig.*, 844 F. Supp. 2d 1040, 1049-50 (2012).
[16] *Id.* at 1054-1056.
[17] *Id.* at 1056-1060.

The court ruled against plaintiffs' Wiretap Act claims, because Apple had not intercepted the content of any communications containing plaintiffs' personal information. As to plaintiff's invasion of privacy claim, the court concluded that the disclosure of personal data was not an "egregious breach" sufficient to give rise to a constitutional claim. The court also ruled that plaintiffs could not bring a claim under the CFAA because they had not shown that their devices were accessed without authorization (having voluntarily installed the apps) and had not established a sufficient loss under the law. The court reasoned that plaintiffs' loss of personal information is not economic damages under the CFAA.[18]

Although the court dismissed most of the claims in the Apple litigation, it allowed claims under California's Unfair Competition Law and Consumer Legal Remedies Act to go ahead. In late November 2013, the court dismissed the entire lawsuit, in part because consumers had not shown they had read Apple's privacy statements before purchasing the devices and there was no evidence that they "read or relied on any particular Apple misrepresentation regarding privacy."[19]

Google

Google has been the target of several privacy litigations. In 2010, plaintiffs sued Google in class actions relating to its roll out of Google "Buzz"—the same product that led to the settlement with the FTC discussed in Chapter 7. Google settled the lawsuit for $8.5 million to be donated to Internet privacy and education organizations.[20]

In a lawsuit filed in 2012, plaintiffs alleged that Google had violated the Wiretap Act and various California laws by combining its former seventy separate privacy policies into a single universal policy allowing Google to use personal information across multiple Google products. Under its new universal policy, Google could combine information from a user's Gmail account with information from a consumer's search inquiries.

---

[18] *Id.* at 1061-1069.
[19] Wendy Davis, *iPhone Users Lose Privacy Lawsuit Against Apple*, Online Media Daily, Nov. 26, 2013, http://www.mediapost.com/publications/article/214346/iphone-users-lose-privacy-lawsuit-against-apple.html.
[20] Chloe Albanesisus, *Google Settles Buzz Class-Action Suit for $8.5M*, PCMAG.com, Sept. 3, 2010, http://www.pcmag.com/article2/0,2817,2368714,00.asp.

The court threw out the case because plaintiffs could not show that they had Article III standing. The court reasoned that the users' claim that they would have to replace their Android phones because of consolidation of privacy policies was speculative because no user said that he or she had in fact bought a replacement phone. Plaintiffs also did not claim that Google was intercepting any information that it did not already possess or had exceeded the limitations on use of such information imposed by its privacy policies.[21] Google has filed a second motion to dismiss the remaining claims, but the court has not ruled on that motion.

In a third privacy action, plaintiffs sued Google for collecting personal information, including names, gender, ZIP codes, GPS data, and phones' universally unique device identifiers (UDIDs), through its Android operating system. Plaintiffs brought claims under the Computer Fraud and Abuse Act, California law, the California Constitutional right to privacy, and other state and common law claims. Not surprisingly, Google argued that plaintiffs did not have standing under Article III.[22]

After a thorough examination, the court concluded that plaintiffs did not have standing. The court ruled that plaintiffs' claim that there was a market for personal information was insufficient to connect Google to the alleged harms. Plaintiffs did not claim that they had tried to sell their personal information, but only that they would either do so in the future or that they had been prevented from entering into a "value for value transaction relating to their [personal information], as a result of the Google Defendants' conduct."

The court also found that plaintiffs' claims that they were injured because they had overpaid for their Android devices and had incurred costs because of Google's conduct were insufficient. However, the court found that the claims that plaintiffs had suffered diminished battery capacity gave them Article III standing.[23]

---

[21] *In re Google, Inc. Privacy Policy Litigation*, No. C 12-01382 PSG, 2012 WL 6738343 (N.D. Cal. Dec. 28, 2012) (order granting defendant's motion to dismiss with leave to amend).
[22] *In re Google Android Consumer Privacy Litig.*, 11-MD-02264 JSW, 2013 WL 1283236 (N.D. Cal. Mar. 26, 2013).
[23] *Id.*

Although the court concluded that the diminished battery life allegations were sufficient for standing, it dismissed the plaintiffs' CFAA claims because there were insufficient facts to show that plaintiffs had been injured. After looking at the remaining claims, the court decided that the plaintiffs could go ahead on some of the state law claims and threw out the remainder of claims, but gave plaintiffs a chance to correct the defects.

In a final Google privacy action, in which plaintiffs claimed that Google had violated anti-wiretapping laws in operating its Gmail service, the court found that the plaintiffs could proceed with those claims.[24] The court rejected Google's argument that its scanning of e-mails to provide targeted advertising fell within the "ordinary course of business" exception under the Wiretap Act and that plaintiffs had consented to interception of their e-mails by signing up for Gmail. The court found that the "ordinary course of business" exception was "narrow" and would only apply "if the alleged interceptions were an instrumental part of the transmission of email."[25]

The ruling attracted considerable attention because of the alleged lack of compatibility between the 1986 anti-wiretapping law and modern technology, including targeted advertising.[26] Google's position in the case also was controversial, because it claimed that users had no legitimate expectation of privacy in their e-mails.[27]

Privacy Litigation Settlements

As already mentioned in conjunction with the AOL and Google litigations, some companies choose to settle rather than litigate privacy lawsuits. Settlement negotiations are normally confidential so the reason for settlement is usually unknown. Likely reasons include a desire to avoid adverse publicity, stop expensive defense costs, and staunch

---

[24] *In re Google Inc.*, 13-MD-02430-LHK, 2013 WL 5423918 (N.D. Cal. Sept. 26, 2013).
[25] *Id.* at 13.
[26] *See* Allison Grande, *Google's Email Setback Hands Weapon to Privacy Plaintiffs*, LAW360 (Sept. 27, 2013), http://www.law360.com/privacy/articles/476411?nl_pk=7fca6e6f-c55b-4225-9d54-6bbc8eca6a30&utm_source=newsletter&utm_medium=email&utm_campaign=privacy.
[27] Steven Musil, *Google filing says Gmail users have no expectation of privacy*, CNET.COM, Aug. 13, 2013, http://news.cnet.com/8301-1023_3-57598420-93/google-filing-says-gmail-users-have-no-expectation-of-privacy/.

diversion of company resources. Where a court has made negative decisions against the defendant, as in the AOL case, the company may also wish to settle to avoid losing at trial or creating negative precedents. Although it is not surprising that privacy cases do not go to trial, settlements also present practical challenges for the parties. One is the difficulty of calculating damages for class members, particularly where the damages of an individual class member are so low that the costs to manage the settlement would be greater than the payments to the member. Lawsuits against Facebook and Google illustrate this point.

Facebook in 2007 launched its "Beacon" program, which updated members' pages to say that they had taken actions, such as renting videos, on websites belonging to companies that participated in the program.[28] Although Facebook soon ended the program, plaintiffs sued the company for violation of privacy rights on the grounds that they had not given consent. Rather than continue to litigate the matter, the parties reached a settlement in 2009 that required Facebook to permanently stop the Beacon program and pay a total of $9.5 million, $3 million of which went to plaintiffs' attorneys and $6.5 million to set up a new charity organization called the Digital Trust Foundation. The 3,663,651 class members received no monetary payment under the settlement.[29]

The court approved the settlement on the grounds that it was "fair, reasonable, and inadequate" under the doctrine of *cy pres*, which is a settlement structure where class action members receive an "indirect benefit" (usually through defendant donations to a third party) rather than a direct monetary payment. The Ninth Circuit confirmed the settlement, in part because distributions to the class members would be "infeasible" given the small amount of damages of each member and the difficulty of proving damages at trial.[30]

A judge in the appeal dissented on the basis that the "settlement perverts the class action into a device for depriving of remedies for wrongs, while enriching both the wrongdoers and the lawyers purporting to represent the class."[31] An objector to the settlement appealed to the Supreme Court

---

[28] *See Lane v. Facebook, Inc.*, 696 F.3d 811, 816-17 (9th Cir. 2012).
[29] *Id.* 817-18.
[30] *Id.* 821-22.
[31] *Id.* 826-27 (Judge Kleinfeld, dissenting).

arguing the settlement is improper because class members will receive nothing under the settlement, but the Court refused to hear the appeal.[32]

Objectors raised similar points against a settlement of a case where Google incorporated words from users' searches into the URL of a results page. In the case, plaintiffs claimed that the search terms in the URLs included personal or identifying information from the search terms. After several years of litigation, Google agreed to settle the matter for $8.5 million, including millions paid to organizations to "promote public awareness and education, and/or to support research, development, and initiatives, related to protecting privacy on the Internet."[33]

Several privacy organizations challenged the settlement because it did not require Google to change its business practices, arguing that it "is absurd to argue that a benefit is provided to the Class where the company makes no material change in its business practices and is allowed to continue the practice that provides the basis for the putative class action."[34]

Practical Implications of Privacy Litigation

The cases discussed illustrate current trends in privacy litigation that may affect both the prosecution and defense of the lawsuits. As noted, establishing standing is generally the first hurdle for those bringing the lawsuit. Although plaintiffs may be aggrieved by a company's sharing data with an advertiser, changes in privacy policies, and display of their images on a social networking site, they may not be able to show that they have a sufficient stake in the lawsuit to have it heard by a court.

A second practical challenge is finding a legal theory that can pass muster. Plaintiffs have tried to bring privacy lawsuits under a wide variety of legal

---

[32] Brief of Petitioner for Writ of Certiorari *Marek v. Facebook* (No. 13-136), *available at* http://blogs.reuters.com/alison-frankel/files/2013/07/marekvlane-certpetition.pdf.   *See Marek v. Lane*, 134 S.Ct. 8 (Mem) (2013) (statement of Chief Justice Roberts respecting the denial of certiorari).

[33] Privacy and Data Security Law Resource Center, *Google Agrees to Pay $8.5 Million to Settle Claims it Disclosed Internet Search Queries*, BLOOMBERG BNA, Jul. 29, 2013, http://www.bna.com/google-agrees-pay-n17179875501/.

[34] Letter from Privacy Organizations to Hon. Edward J. Davila (Aug. 22, 2013), *available at* http://www.consumerwatchdog.org/resources/ltrgooglereferrer082213.pdf.

theories, including the Wiretap Act, the Stored Communications Act, the Electronic Communications Protection Act, trademark law and state laws, but often have been unable to show that their claims meet these laws. A typical issue a plaintiff faces is that many of the laws, such as the Wiretap Act, predate modern technology such as the Internet and are not an easy fit for the facts and circumstances of the case.

A related practical challenge is damages. Damages in privacy lawsuits are often difficult to prove because of problems in quantifying or articulating harm to privacy. A plaintiff may not like having his or her data shared, but still may not be able to show that the data has monetary value or that he or she was harmed by the sharing.

Courts generally have not been receptive to arguments that personal data has inherent value, because there is no established market for such data. Plaintiffs have had some success in getting around this problem by alleging more concrete harms, such as diminished battery life, increased purchasing prices for devices, and diminished bandwidth, but these theories have not yet been tested at trial. Settlements of privacy litigations have also confronted challenges in articulating damages for class members and have resorted to making payments to charitable or public interest organizations, rather than class members.

Defendants also are challenged by the expense, diversion of resources, and the negative publicity that can result from claims that a business has not respected privacy. Although defendants have had successes in some privacy litigations, plaintiffs and their lawyers are becoming adept at overcoming hurdles of standing and damages. As seen in the recent Google Gmail case, plaintiffs have also had some success in framing privacy claims relating to common Internet practices, such as targeted advertising, under laws such as the Wiretap Act. Because privacy lawsuits are unlikely to disappear, businesses potentially subject to being sued should carefully assess their practices to diminish risk.

9

Surveillance and Privacy

United States laws relating to government surveillance occupy a different space than most federal data privacy and security laws. Unlike other laws, surveillance involves direct government action, not collection of data by a business or unauthorized access to communications by a private party. The government is also subject to constitutional restraints, including the Fourth Amendment. Moreover, distrust of government authority may stimulate a stronger public response than collection of personal data by private businesses, including comparisons to Orwell's "Big Brother" and the practices of totalitarian regimes.

Discussion of government surveillance and the relating constitutional and policy debates are nonetheless important topics in a book that discusses emerging trends in the field of privacy and security that may affect future legislation and best practices. As recent history shows, attitudes toward surveillance may affect views about other aspects of privacy and data security, including collection of personal information by businesses.

Surveillance Under US Law

Surveillance is a pervasive part of our security-conscious world. Closed Circuit Television Cameras (CCTV) installed by private businesses record pictures of people on sidewalks, in stores, and in public places. GPS devices, including those embedded in smart phones, allow geographic tracking of crime suspects. Advances in face recognition technology may also soon make it possible for computers to identify people in a crowd by their faces.[1] Surveillance information obtained

---

[1] Charlie Savage, *Facial Scanning is Making Gains in Surveillance*, N.Y. TIMES, Aug. 21, 2013, *available at* http://www.nytimes.com/2013/08/21/us/facial-scanning-is-making-gains-in-surveillance.html?_r=0.

from private enterprises can be of considerable value to law enforcement authorities, as shown by the videos that led to the identification of the Boston Marathon bombers.

Government surveillance is not only used for detecting criminal activities, such as surveillance of a suspect, but also for non-criminal purposes, including monitoring perceived domestic threats. Non-criminal surveillance has a controversial history. In the 1960s and 1970s, the US government, at the behest of the president and/or FBI, conducted domestic surveillance of communists, anti-war protesters, and civil rights activists through warrantless searches and electronic eavesdropping.

One well-known example is the FBI's wiretapping and surveillance of Dr. Martin Luther King, Jr. from 1958 to his death, which was used to blackmail Dr. King. Revelations about these domestic surveillance activities gave rise to investigations into the privacy invasions of US citizens in the late 1970s. The investigations of the Senate's Church Committee into domestic spying led to enactment in 1978 of the Foreign Intelligence Surveillance Act (FISA).[2] Along with the "Patriot Act," enacted shortly after the September 11, 2001 terrorist attacks, FISA is the legal underpinning of domestic non-criminal surveillance in the United States.[3]

FISA established for the first time legal procedures for gathering "foreign intelligence" information in the United States from "foreign powers" and "agents of foreign powers," including US citizens and permanent residents. Under FISA, non-criminal electronic surveillance within the United States may only be used to collect information needed to protect the United States against attacks by foreign powers, sabotage, international terrorism or clandestine intelligence activities.[4] FISA established a procedure whereby the attorney general certifies under seal to the Foreign Intelligence Surveillance Court (FISC) the necessity to conduct surveillance of a foreign power, including groups engaged in international terrorism or the "international proliferation of weapons of mass destruction."[5]

---

[2] 50 U.S.C. §§ 1801 *et seq.* (West).
[3] *See* GEOFFREY R. STONE, PERILOUS TIMES: FREE SPEECH IN WARTIME FROM THE SEDITION ACT OF 1798 TO THE WAR ON TERRORISM *passim* (W.W. Norton, 2005).
[4] 50 U.S.C. § 1801(a)-(b) & (e); 50 U.S.C. § 1802 (West).
[5] *Id.*

Section 702, which was added to FISA in 2008, authorizes the NSA to collect "communications by foreign persons that utilize U.S. communications providers."[6] Under the authority of Section 702, the attorney general and the director of National Intelligence prepare written certifications to the FISC to get foreign intelligence information. After receiving an order from the FISC, the government may authorize up to one year of targeting of non-United States persons "reasonably believed to be located overseas to acquire foreign intelligence information." The NSA says that "[t]he collection is acquired through compelled assistance from relevant electronic communications service providers."[7]

Collection of information is also conducted under the "business records" section of FISA, generally referred to as Section 215 of the Patriot Act.[8] Section 215 authorizes the FBI to make an application for an order producing documents or other things "for an investigation to obtain foreign intelligence information not concerning a United States person or to protect against international terrorism or clandestine intelligence activities, provided that such investigation of a United States person is not conducted solely upon the basis of activities protected by the first amendment of the Constitution."[9] The application must include a "statement of facts showing that there are reasonable grounds to believe that the tangible things sought are relevant to an authorized investigation" and that the investigation is being conducted under guidelines approved by the attorney general.[10]

Non-public FISC orders issued under Section 215 require US telecommunications providers to provide the NSA with information about telephone calls to, from, or within the United States known as "telephony metadata."[11] The NSA states that telephony metadata consists of information "such as the called and calling telephone numbers and the date, time, and duration of the call – but no user identification, content, or cell site

---

[6] 50 U.S.C. §§ 1881 *et seq.* (West); *see also* National Security Agency, *The National Security Agency: Missions, Authorities, Oversight and Partnerships* [hereinafter NSA Missions] 3-4, Aug. 9, 2013, http://www.nsa.gov/public_info/_files/speeches_testimonies/2013_08_09_the_nsa_story.pdf.

[7] *See NSA Missions supra* n. 6 at 4.

[8] 50 U.S.C. § 1861 (West).

[9] 50 U.S.C. § 1861(a)(1).

[10] 50 U.S.C. § 1861(b)(2)(A) & (a)(2)(A).

[11] *See NSA Missions supra* n. 6 at 5.

location data. The purpose of this particular collection is to identify the U.S. nexus of a foreign terrorist threat to the homeland."[12] Telephony metadata must be associated with a "seed identifier," such as a telephone number, used to query the telephony metadata. There must also be a "reasonable, articulable suspicion" that the seed identifier is associated with a foreign terrorist organization previously identified to and approved by the FISC.[13] If the "seed identifier" is a US person, "the suspicion of an association with a particular foreign terrorist organization cannot be based solely on activities protected by the First Amendment."[14]

FISC first authorized the Section 215 program in 2006 and has subsequently approved the program thirty-four times.[15] The Obama Administration states that information about collection of information under Section 215 was "made available to all Members of Congress and Congress reauthorized Section 215 without change after this information was provided."[16] The program is subject to oversight by the Department of Justice, the Director of National Intelligence, the FISC, and internal review by the NSA.[17]

The NSA Controversy

On June 5, 2013, the UK's *Guardian* newspaper published a story stating that the NSA was collecting "telephone records" of millions of US customers of Verizon under a "top secret" order of FISC issued under Section 215.[18] The next day the *Guardian* published a story about the NSA "Prism" program claiming that the program gave the NSA "direct access to servers of firms including Google, Apple and Facebook."[19] All the

---

[12] *Id.*

[13] *Id.*

[14] *Id.*

[15] The White House, *Bulk Collection of Telephony Metadata Under Section 215 of the Patriot Act* [hereinafter White House Bulk Collection] 1, Aug. 9, 2013, http://big.assets.huffington post.com/Section215.pdf.

[16] *Id.* at 2.

[17] *Id.* at 5.

[18] Glenn Greenwald, *NSA Collecting Phone Records of Millions of Verizon Customers Daily*, GUARDIAN, Jun. 5, 2013, *available at* http://www.theguardian.com/ world/2013/jun/06/nsa-phone-records-verizon-court-order.

[19] Glenn Greenwald & Ewen MacAskill, *NSA Prism program taps in to user data of Apple, Google and others*, GUARDIAN. Jun. 6, 2013, *available at* http://www.theguardian.com/world/ 2013/jun/06/us-tech-giants-nsa-data.

companies referenced in the report denied knowledge of the program.[20] On June 9, 2013, the *Guardian* revealed that the "whistleblower" leaking the documents was Edward Snowden, who had formerly been employed as an infrastructure analyst by a contractor to the NSA. Snowden said that he had made these revelations because "I don't want to live in a society that does these sorts of things."[21]

Snowden's first revelations were followed by publication of other NSA documents and by Snowden's flight from Hong Kong to Russia, which granted him temporary asylum. On June 21, 2013, federal prosecutors filed a criminal complaint against Snowden for theft, "unauthorized communication of national defense information," and "willful communication of classified communications intelligence information to an unauthorized person" under the US Espionage Act.[22]

Snowden's revelation of top secret documents about NSA programs prompted starkly diverse reactions. In the "Snowden is a Traitor" camp were House Speaker John Boehner and Senators Dianne Feinstein and Bill Nelson, who claimed that he had jeopardized security programs that "keep Americans safe."[23] On the "Snowden is a Patriot" side were those who praised his actions because "his leaks led to more open debate and more democratic process than would've existed otherwise."[24]

The Constitutionality of US Government Surveillance

The NSA controversy ignited not only divergent views about Snowden's acts, but a debate over the constitutionality of the surveillance programs.

---

[20] *Id.*

[21] Glenn Greenwald, *NSA Whistleblower Edward Snowden: "I Don't Want to Live in a Society that Does These Sort of Things" – Video*, GUARDIAN, Jun. 9, 2013, *available at* http://www.theguardian.com/world/video/2013/jun/09/nsa-whistleblower-edward-snowden-interview-video.

[22] Peter Finn & Sari Horwitz, *U.S. charges Snowden with espionage*, WASH. POST, Jun. 21, 2013, *available at* http://www.washingtonpost.com/ world/national-security/us-charges-snowden-with-espionage/2013/06/21/507497d8-dab1-11e2-a016-92547bf094cc_story.html.

[23] Brett LoGiurato, *John Boehner: Edward Snowden is a "Traitor*,*"* S.F. CHRONICLE, Jun. 11, 2013, http://www.sfgate.com/technology/ businessinsider/article/JOHN-BOEHNER-Edward-Snowden-Is-A-Traitor-4593261.php.

[24] Ezra Klein, *Edward Snowden, Patriot*, WASH. POST, Aug. 9, 2013, *available at* http://www.washingtonpost.com/blogs/wonkblog/wp/2013/08/09/edward-snowden-patriot/.

On the same day that the president announced reforms to the programs, the White House released a defense of the constitutionality of "Bulk Collection of Telephony Metadata under Section 215 of the USA Patriot Act." The Obama Administration claimed that the program was constitutional under the Fourth Amendment because collection of metadata is not a "search" because "participants in telephone calls lack a reasonable expectation of privacy for purposes of the Fourth Amendment in the telephone numbers used to make and receive their calls."[25]

The administration's support for this argument is the 1979 Supreme Court case of *Smith v. Maryland* in which the police placed a "pen register" on the telephone of a suspect recording the numbers he called as part of an investigation into a robbery. When the register displayed the number of a victim, the police arrested the suspect. The Supreme Court concluded in the case that the recording of the information was not a "search" because a telephone user voluntarily turns over information to a third party—the telephone company. The Supreme Court also wrote that the user has "assumed the risk that the company would reveal to the police the numbers [] dialed."[26]

The White House argued that the NSA programs also did not violate the First Amendment because the government did not collect the content of the calls and because its collection is "in furtherance of the compelling national interest in identifying and tracking terrorist operatives and ultimately in thwarting terrorist attacks, particularly against the United States."[27]

Some privacy advocates disagree with the administration's argument. They counter that the *Smith* case and the "third party" doctrine for which it stands do not apply to NSA practices because the *Smith* case involved a single pen register—not a massive collection of metadata. *Smith*, they say, was decided in an era where privacy expectations were far different because the ability to collect and analyze massive amounts of digital metadata did not yet exist. As Senator Mike Lee said in questioning the then head of the FBI about the program, "[t]he technologies that are at issue now didn't exist then – certainly weren't even contemplated then....

---

[25] *See White House Bulk Collection supra* n. 15 at 2.
[26] *Smith v. Maryland*, 442 U.S. 735, 744 (1979).
[27] *See White House Bulk Collection supra* n. 15 at 22.

And the more you aggregate large quantities of metadata potentially on every single American citizen and you give someone with the executive branch of government the power to search all of that, you do give them a pretty broad view into the lives of the American people...[and] you start to breach a reasonable expectation of privacy[.]"[28]

Critics of the NSA programs also argue that the programs violate modern expectations of privacy by "chilling" First Amendment rights of speech and association. Pointing to US Supreme Court Justice Sotomayor's concurrence in *United States v. Jones*, they say that government surveillance places people at a significant disadvantage. Justice Sotomayor wrote in *Jones* that "the Government's unrestrained power to assemble data that reveal private aspects of identity is susceptible to abuse" and that it "may 'alter the relationship between citizen and government in a way that is inimical to democratic society.'" Justice Sotomayor also wrote that "the existence of a reasonable societal expectation of privacy" may be affected by whether "people reasonably expect that their movements will be recorded and aggregated in a manner that enables the Government to ascertain, more or less at will, their political and religious belief, sexual habits, and so on."[29]

Justice Sotomayor's view does not necessarily reflect that of the Supreme Court if and when a constitutional challenge is mounted against government surveillance. However it rules, the Supreme Court's views about the shifting contours of a "reasonable expectation of privacy" under the Fourth Amendment will likely have ramifications on broader issues about collection of personal data by private enterprises.

The "Snowden Effect"

The NSA controversy has had a spillover effect on privacy and security sometimes called the "Snowden Effect." Three aspects of this effect may affect the contours of future legal developments.

---

[28] Pema Levy, *NSA Controversy: The Supreme Court Case that Could Determine the Fate of NSA Surveillance*, INT'L BUS. TIMES, Jul. 15, 2013, http://www.ibtimes.com/nsa-controversy-supreme-court-case-could-determine-fate-nsa-surveillance-1344567.

[29] *United States v. Jones*, 132 S. Ct. 945, 956 (Sotomayor, J., concurring).

Data Collection Practices and Surveillance

Some have used revelations about the NSA surveillance programs to question whether people have implicitly enabled surveillance by entrusting large amounts of personal data to businesses, particularly on the Internet. In an *Economist* article titled "Should the Government Know Less than Google?" journalist Matt Steinglass pointed out that "[i]n the online world, essentially everything we do is always being archived and searched by the companies that provide us access...The problem isn't so much that we haven't set up a legal architecture to preserve our online privacy from the government; it's that we haven't set up a legal architecture to preserve our online privacy from *anyone at all*. If we don't have laws and regulations that create meaningful zones of online privacy from corporations, the attempt to create online privacy from the government will be an absurdity."[30]

Others disagree, pointing to the differences between the powers of the US government and private enterprise. Businesses like Facebook and Google do not compel consumers to use them, but instead provide free services in return for personal information. Private companies are powerful, but do not have the FBI and NSA to back them up.

Although business collection is different from government access to data, the NSA controversy has brought about calls for increased transparency about data collected by private enterprises. FTC Commissioner Julie Brill wrote in a *Washington Post* op-ed that the NSA revelations have given "consumers...a crash course in the price we pay to participate in the online and mobile marketplace: Our most intimate information floats free in cyberspace, ripe for any data miner – government or otherwise–to collect, use, package and sell."[31] Commissioner Brill urged commercial data brokers to be transparent about what they learn about consumers "from the cookies that hitch rides as users travel online and from the

---

[30] M[att] S[teinglass], *Should the Government Know Less than Google?* THE ECONOMIST, June 11, 2013, http://www.economist.com/blogs/democracyinamerica/2013/06/surveillance-0 (emphasis in original).
[31] Julie Brill, *Demanding Transparency from Data Brokers*, WASH. POST, Aug. 15, 2013, http://articles.washingtonpost.com/2013-08-15/opinions/41412540_1_data-brokers-fair-credit-reporting-act-data-fuel.

social media sites where we post everything from home addresses to pictures to magazine subscriptions and store purchases, as well as deeds on file in towns and counties."[32]

Commissioner Brill's statements prompted a strong riposte from the DMA—a trade association promoting data-driven marketing. The DMA responded that the data shared by consumers provides many benefits, including "fuel[ing] popular, beneficial and harmless services that consumers want – even demand – as part of their digital lifestyles."[33] The DMA also complained that Commissioner Brill's "op-ed demonizes data and conflates the activities of the National Security Agency (NSA) with those of responsible data-driven marketers" and that "surveillance issues" are distinct from "commercial uses of data."[34]

The Privacy/Security Tradeoff

A second aspect of the Snowden Effect is a renewed debate about the alleged tradeoff between security and privacy in the post-9/11 world. President Obama encapsulated this view when he responded to a question about the NSA by stating, "I think it is important to recognize that you can't have 100 per cent security and then also have 100 per cent privacy and zero inconvenience. You know, we are going to have to make some choices as a society."[35]

Privacy advocates respond that the security/privacy argument sets a false equation involving two disparate concepts. The formulation, according to Torin Monahan, the editor of *Surveillance and Society*, "implies that a diminishment in one is an increase in the other, and that's not empirically accurate. Every time we give up privacy doesn't mean we're increasing our security, or vice-versa."[36]

---

[32] *Id.*

[33] Susan Taplinger, *DMA Responds to Op-Ed Attacking Commercial Data Use*, Direct Marketing Ass'n Official Blog, Aug. 19, 2013, http://blog.thedma.org/ 2013/08/19/dma-responds-to-op-ed-attacking-commercial-data-use/.

[34] *Id.*

[35] Michael Pearson, *Obama: No One Listening to Your Calls*, CNN.com, June 9, 2013, http://www.cnn.com/2013/06/07/politics/nsa-data-mining/index.html.

[36] Marc Herman, *A Security Scholar Talks about the NSA Scandal*, PAC. STAND., Jun. 11, 2013, http://www.psmag.com/politics/a-security-scholar-talks-the-nsa-scandal-59964/.

The security/privacy equation, if inexact, highlights important issues about public perceptions of data collection by businesses. In the light of the NSA revelations, the US House of Representatives came close to overturning a key aspect of the legal surveillance framework. Public attitudes are also changing, as shown by an opinion survey conducted a month after the revelations that found that "[n]early three-quarters of Americans say the NSA programs are infringing on some Americans' privacy rights, and about half see those programs as encroaching on their own privacy."[37] The further ramifications of public attitudes are difficult to predict, but the controversy has already stimulated greater debate about the topic than any time since the Patriot Act was enacted and may lead to substantive changes in privacy and surveillance laws.

The "Nothing to Hide" Argument

A final aspect of the Snowden Effect is the effect the NSA controversy has had on debates about the meaning of privacy in a digital and interconnected world. As John Cassidy wrote in *The New Yorker*, the Snowden affair "isn't primarily a matter of whether U.S. laws were broken. It's a much larger issue of how far privacy extends in the Internet age, and how the rights of the individual should be balanced against the government's obligation to counter terrorism and other threats."[38]

For some, privacy should not be used to hide information that could protect us from internal and external enemies. If one has nothing to hide, the argument goes, why be concerned about government surveillance, if one has willingly provided information to Verizon, Google, or Facebook?[39] Judge Richard Posner advanced a similar view when he said that "'[w]hen people today decry lack of privacy, what they want, I think, is mainly something quite different from seclusion; they want

---

[37] Jon Cohen & Dan Balz, *Poll: Privacy Concerns Rise after NSA leaks*, WASH. POST, Jul. 23, 2013, *available at* http://www.washingtonpost.com/politics/poll-privacy-concerns-rise-after-nsa-leaks/2013/07/23/3a1b64a6-f3c7-11e2-a2f1-a7acf9bd5d3a_story.html.

[38] John Cassidy, *Snowden's Legacy: A Public Debate about Online Privacy*, NEW YORKER, Aug. 20, 2013, http://www.newyorker.com/online/blogs/ johncassidy/2013/08/snowdens-legacy-public-debate-about-online-privacy.html.

[39] *See* Daniel J. Solove, *"I've Got Nothing to Hide" and Other Misunderstandings of Privacy*, 44 SAN DIEGO LAW REVIEW 745 (2007); DANIEL J. SOLOVE, NOTHING TO HIDE: THE FALSE TRADEOFF BETWEEN PRIVACY AND SECURITY, *passim* (Yale University Press, 2011).

more power to conceal information about themselves that others might use to their disadvantage.'"[40]

In the view of Daniel J. Solove, a privacy scholar who has written extensively on this subject, the "nothing to hide" argument focuses too narrowly on privacy as secrecy, while ignoring other aspects of privacy, including the social value of privacy and the disintegration of the social fabric that occurs when privacy is eroded or eliminated. While surveillance is often described in reference to Orwell's "Big Brother," a more apt literary allusion, according to Solove, may be Franz Kafka's novel *The Trial*, "which depicts a bureaucracy with inscrutable purposes that uses people's information to make important decisions about them, yet denies the people the ability to participate in how their information is used."[41]

The debate over NSA surveillance may not resolve the debate between privacy as unwarranted secrecy and as a positive social value, but will likely continue to stimulate proposals that may affect the law and businesses' data collection activities.

---

[40] *See Solove supra* n. 39 *"I Have Got Nothing to Hide"* at 751, quoting RICHARD A. POSNER, THE ECONOMICS OF JUSTICE 271 (Harvard University Press, 1983).
[41] *Id.* at 756.

10

Privacy and Security Trends

The privacy and data security ecosystem is rapidly evolving. Just as the growth of the Internet and the debate over government surveillance has affected the legal contours of these fields, changing technology will likely produce future changes to law and best practices. Because of these ongoing developments, close attention should be paid to emerging trends affecting legal compliance and risk management.

Big Data

"Big Data" is a term that has gained currency in recent years. Although not precise, Big Data generally refers to the ability to sort and organize massive amounts of unstructured data from multiple sources in a short period of time. Big Data can also refer to the ability to find patterns or results from large amounts of data or to data sets so large and unstructured that they cannot be handled by traditional database tools.

Big Data is feasible because of the technological ability to collect and cheaply store large amounts of data from a great variety of sources, including sensors, Internet searches, social media postings, transaction records, text messages, e-mails, and GPS signals. It is estimated that the world creates 2.5 quintillion bytes of data a day.[1] On Facebook alone, 350 million photos are uploaded and there are 4.5 billion "likes" a day.[2]

---

[1] IBM, *What is Big Data*, http://www.ibm.com/big-data/us/en/.
[2] Craig Smith, *By the Numbers: 87 Amazing Facebook Stats,* Digital Marketing Ramblings, Aug. 25, 2013, http://expandedramblings.com/index.php/by-the-numbers-17-amazing-facebook-stats/.

Given the amount of data that is being created and compiled by companies, a Big Data set may be as large as an exabyte—which is a quintillion (10^{18}) bytes. As a point of comparison, it has been estimated that all words ever spoken by human beings amount to 5 exabytes.[3]

Big Data has both proponents and critics. Big Data supporters believe it will confer benefits on consumers and businesses including allowing discovery of previously unknown associations and patterns from unstructured information, such as the drug interactions mentioned earlier. IBM, which is active in the field, promotes the use of Big Data for decision making, gaining "full understanding of customers," expanding cyber security and intelligence operations, analyzing data for improved business results, and "increas[ing] operational efficiency."[4]

Some privacy advocates are concerned with the potential loss of control by consumers that may result from Big Data. As more and more data is collected through devices of all sorts and maintained and stored in multiple locations, consumers may have little or no sense of where their data is located and how and by whom it is being used or processed. Control and transparency issues may be exacerbated if the data concerns sensitive issues such as medical conditions, is being used for a purpose other than that for which it was collected, or is gathered without a person's knowledge. Big Data critics also worry about the lack of legal accountability for gathering and use of data and the difficulties of consumer access or correction of data. A final concern is security risk – with Big Data comes Big Security issues, particularly because massive amounts of data may be cheaply stored for indefinite periods of time.

As with other aspects of the ongoing evolution in the ways in which data is being collected and used, the future of Big Data may be affected by government access to information gathered and maintained by private enterprise. This confluence of "Big Data" and "Big Brother" could create challenges for those who collect data from consumers and prompt further

---

[3] Julian Bunn, *How Big is a Petabyte, Exabyte, Zettabyte or a Yottabyte?* High Scalability, Sept. 11, 2012, http://highscalability.com/blog/2012/9/11/how-big-is-a-petabyte-exabyte-zettabyte-or-a-yottabyte.html.

[4] IBM, *The 5 Game Changing Big Data Use Cases*, http://www-01.ibm.com/software/data/bigdata/use-cases.html.

calls for greater transparency or more effective anonymization of the data to prevent linkage to identifiable persons.

Cloud Computing

Data privacy and security are also affected by the practice of entrusting large amounts of personal information and other data to remote storage or processing facilities colloquially referred to as the "cloud." "Cloud computing," like Big Data, is not a precise term. As generally used, cloud computing refers to the storage or processing of data in a location other than the user's computer system and with an Internet interface facilitating access from multiple locations and devices. Both software and storage services are typically managed by a third party called a "cloud computing provider." Enterprises use cloud computing as part of a distributed business model to increase flexibility and scalability, lower costs, and allow access from multiple locations or devices.

One familiar consumer cloud storage application is Apple's iCloud, which is built into Apple devices to allow users to store and access music, photos, calendars, and documents from multiple devices. An example of cloud software is Google Apps for Business, which allows users to access tools such as e-mail, calendars, and presentation and word processing from a device without installing software on the device. Other familiar cloud applications include Dropbox, GoToMeeting, Microsoft Office 365, GoogleDocs, and Carbonite.

Cloud computing creates potential privacy and data security issues. One important issue is control of data. Because data is being stored or "hosted" remotely—sometimes in multiple locations and data centers—a cloud computing provider has access to data and is in charge of its security. Potential privacy implications may ensue, because "owners" of data generally have legal responsibilities to maintain the privacy and security of data and cloud computing providers may seek to avoid liability for storage of data through their agreements with owners.

Those responsible for security and privacy of data need to be aware of and analyze the risks connected to cloud computing and mitigate those risks through due diligence and contractual provisions. Enterprises engaging cloud computing providers also need to know "how, where and by whom the data is being processed/sub-processed."[5] Because cloud computing may affect the ability of consumers to access and correct data, data owners should consider giving consumers greater information as to where data is located or processed.

If there is a breach of privacy or security, issues may arise as to whether the client or the hosting party is responsible for data stored on the cloud. Cloud computing providers do not own the data that they are hosting, but are instead providing a contracted service. Although data owners are normally responsible for reporting security breaches, some laws, including California's data breach notification law, require businesses maintaining personal data that they do not own to notify the data owner "immediately following discovery" of a breach.[6] In addition, businesses using cloud providers need to be aware of liability limitations that providers normally require exempting them from damages for the data. As with other third parties, cloud providers should be carefully vetted in regard to the security measures that they maintain.

As discussed in Chapter 4, the transfer of data to hosting companies may be affected by restrictions placed on data transfers in some jurisdictions, including the European Union. As with Big Data, the NSA controversy could also affect cloud computing because of concerns that data stored or transferred to US cloud providers may be accessed by the US government. Indeed, it has been estimated that the US cloud computing industry may lose $22 to $35 billion over the next three years because of the reluctance to entrust data to US cloud providers.[7]

"Do Not Track" (DNT) Technology

Do Not Track or DNT is a proposed http header built into Internet browsers to ask a website to disable its tracking of a consumer for advertising

---

[5] Article 29 Data Protection Working Party, *Opinion 05/2012 on Cloud Computing*, 2, Jul. 1, 2012, http://ec.europa.eu/justice/data-protection/article-29/documentation/opinion-recommendation/files/2012/wp196_en.pdf.

[6] Ann. Cal. Civ. Code § 1798.82(b) (West).

[7] Katherine Jacobsen, *How the NSA Leaks Could Affect the US Cloud Computing Industry*, CHRISTIAN SCI. MONITOR, Aug. 26, 2013, http://www.csmonitor.com/Innovation/2013/0826/How-the-NSA-leaks-could-affect-the-US-cloud-computing-industry.

purposes. DNT is directed to blocking, at least to some extent, "online behavioral advertising" (OBA) which uses cookies installed when visiting a website to deliver up targeted advertising to consumers from their actions on the website. The White House and the FTC have endorsed DNT as promoting "privacy and consumer choice" by making it easier for consumers to control the tracking of their online activities.[8]

DNT may impact legal developments in the privacy field because it affects a key element of the Internet economy—providing personal information (such as age, sex, and geolocation information) in return for free services (such as social networking or search engines). Consumer advocates and agencies such as the FTC see DNT as a way of putting consumers in the driver's seat as to how their personal data is used for targeted advertising.

The advertising industry, in contrast, is resistant to DNT technology (particularly as a default browser setting), because it prevents consumer choice and may harm the thriving Internet economy. The debate over DNT has reached the World Wide Web Consortium (W3C), which sets standards for how sites should respond to the DNT signals, but has seemingly fallen apart because of disputes among the stakeholders and the difficulties of arriving at an acceptable DNT solution. The result may be that DNT will be put into effect in a different fashion, including legislation or unilateral browser implementation.[9]

California in 2013 amended its Online Privacy Protection Act (CalOPPA) to require operators of websites to state in their privacy policies how they respond to DNT browser signals and to disclose whether third parties collect personal information about consumers' online activities over time and across different sites. This law, which was the first of its kind, has created controversy because DNT mechanisms are in a state of flux and operators may not yet have determined how they will respond to the

---

[8] Federal Trade Commission, *Protecting Consumer Privacy in an Era of Rapid Change: Recommendations for Businesses and Policymakers* 3, 4, Mar. 2012, [hereinafter FTC 2012 Report], http://ftc.gov/os/2012/03/120326privacyreport.pdf.
[9] Sam Pfeile, *Is This the End for DNT? DAA Pulls Out of W3C Process*, PRIVACY ADVISOR, Sept. 17, 2013, https://www.privacyassociation.org/publications/is_this_the_end_for_dnt_daa_pulls_out_of_w3c_process.

signal.[10] Difficulties also exist because operators may not be able to identify the third parties with whom information is shared or because the third parties with whom an entity deals may be constantly changing.[11] Businesses may thus face implementation challenges when the new law becomes effective on January 1, 2014.

Biometrics

Another developing technology that affects data privacy is the collection and use of biometric data. Biometric data consists of unique physiological traits of human beings used for identification, authentication or security purposes. Common biometric identifiers are fingerprints, DNA, iris scans, voice identification, and keyboard strokes. In the future, it may be possible to link video surveillance with face recognition techniques to identify specific individuals. A project currently being tested by the Department of Homeland Security called Biometric Optical Surveillance System (BOSS) seeks to identify a person in a crowd using face recognition technology.[12]

Biometric technology is developing rapidly for a wide variety of uses. Biometric identifiers, such as voice identification, are used to prevent "proxy" test taking—the taking of a test by someone other than the registered test taker.[13] Members of Congress have urged adoption of a national ID card with biometric identifiers, such as a fingerprint, hand scan, or iris scan, to decrease illegal immigration.[14]

Developers have also cited the advantages of combining facial-recognition technology with Google's wearable computer "Google Glass," to allow

---

[10] Dennis Holmes, *What do the New Disclosure Requirements Under CALOPPA Mean for Your Business*, IAPP Privacy Tracker, Oct. 8, 2013, https://www.privacyassociation.org/privacy_tracker/post/what_do_the_new_disclosure_requirements_under_caloppa_mean_for_y our_busines.

[11] *Id.*

[12] Charlie Savage, *Facial Scanning is Making Gains in Surveillance*, N.Y. TIMES, Aug. 21, 2013, http://www.nytimes.com/2013/08/21/us/facial-scanning-is-making-gains-in-surveillance.html?_r=1&.

[13] Leonard Klie, *ETS Adds Voice identification to Increase TOEFL Exam Security*, Jul. 10, 2012, SPEECH TECHNOLOGY, http://www.speechtechmag.com/Articles/Editorial/FYI/ETS-Adds-Voice-identification-to-Increase-TOEFL-Exam-Security-83634.aspx.

[14] Declan McCullagh, *Senators Push Obama for Biometric National ID Card*, CNET Mar. 18, 2010, http://news.cnet.com/8301-13578_3-20000758-38.html.

doctors to verify a patient's identity and instantly bring up medical records.[15] Security and authentication concerns have also been cited as a reason for adopting biometric identification techniques to separate the authorized from the unauthorized.

Biometric identifiers are controversial because of the perceived invasion of the privacy of the bodily features of a person. Unlike some other technologies, biometric identifiers have the capability of providing a direct link to a specific person. Despite their common use as fingerprints for identification, biometric identifiers have also received several negative depictions in popular culture. Often referenced as an example of biometrics run amok is Steven Spielberg's *Minority Report*, where the Tom Cruise character receives targeted advertisements in a store identifying him by name from a retinal scan.

The fear that the government may use face recognition techniques as part of surveillance fuels more privacy concerns.[16] Privacy advocates, such as EPIC, object to biometric identifiers on the ground that surveillance information may be joined with other sensitive personal information to create profiles of people that can be used for improper purposes. Objections are also lodged against biometrics collected under compulsion or without informed consent by the person involved. EU data protection authorities have laid out guidelines to guarantee the security of biometrics and control potential risks from their use, but there are no similar guidelines in the United States.[17]

Because it is a rapidly changing technological field with a wide variety of potential business uses, debates over the use of biometric identifiers are likely to continue to be an active privacy issue.

---

[15] David Talbot, *Google Irks Developers with Ruling on Facial-Recognition Apps*, MIT TECHNOL. R., Jun. 10, 2013, http://www.technologyreview.com/news/515756/google-irks-developers-with-ruling-on-facial-recognition-apps/. As the title of the article shows, Google has banned the use of facial recognition technology because of Congressional pressure.

[16] Electronic Frontier Foundation, *Biometrics*, https://www.eff.org/issues/biometrics.

[17] Article 29 Data Protection Working Party, *Opinion 3/2012 on developments in biometric technologies*, Apr. 27, 2012, http://ec.europa.eu/justice/data-protection/article-29/documentation/opinion-recommendation/files/2012/wp193_en.pdf.

The Internet of Things

The "Internet of Things" (IoT) consists of machines and other devices with sensors or chips that send data to the Internet using communicative technologies, including Radio-Frequency Identification (RFID), wired and wireless connections, and GPS. IoT includes "smart" devices such as mobile telephones, cars, appliances, power meters, medical devices, and even shoes that can communicate with each other and with people. A medical device that monitors a patient's blood sugar levels and sends information to the patient's physician is an example of such a device.[18] IoT is growing exponentially and it is estimated that by 2015 there will be 25 billion connected devices with that number doubling by 2020 and that IoT will produce $4.5 trillion in global revenue by 2020.[19]

Like "Big Data," IoT is cited by many as a beneficial technology that will anticipate and satisfy consumer needs in a highly personalized manner, find efficient solutions to distribution problems, and allow seamless communication both to consumers and third parties, including doctors, utilities, and retailers. Those who are more skeptical of IoT technology have cited privacy and security concerns, including the fear that hackers armed with malware may be able to access "smart devices" to obtain sensitive personal information and the difficulties of providing notice to consumers about commercial uses of IoT technology, such as in retail stores.[20]

Other concerns about IoT include the potential misuse of data by companies and the increased tracking and surveillance made possible by the technology.[21] Recent demonstrations have shown that it is even possible to "hack" a car by accessing its computer system to interfere

---

[18] Press Release, Federal Trade Commission, *FTC Seeks Input on Privacy and Security Implications of the Internet of Things*, Apr. 17, 2013, http://www.ftc.gov/opa/2013/04/internetthings.shtm. The FTC subsequently held a public workshop on IoT on November 19, 2013. *See Internet of Things Privacy & Security in a Connected World*, http://www.ftc.gov/bcp/workshops/internet-of-things/.

[19] Jedidiah Bracy, *The Internet of Things: The Good, the Bad and the Ugly*, IAPP Privacy Perspectives, Jul. 26, 2013, https://www.privacyassociation.org/privacy_perspectives/post/the_internet_of_things_the_good_the_bad_and_the_ugly.

[20] *See Room for Debate: Privacy, When Your Shoes Track Every Step*, N.Y. TIMES, Sept. 9, 2013, http://www.nytimes.com/roomfordebate/2013/09/08/privacy-and-the-internet-of-things.

[21] *Id.*

with operations like steering, the GPS system, and braking.[22] And in an episode of the popular show *Homeland*, terrorists assassinated the vice president by hacking into his pacemaker.[23]

The FTC's recent focus on IoT shows that the privacy and security implications of the technology are gaining greater recognition. On September 4, 2013, the FTC reached a settlement with a home security video camera company that failed to use reasonable security for its products and allowed hackers to display consumers' private camera feeds on the Internet, sometimes with geolocation information. The settlement prohibited the company from misrepresenting "the security of its cameras or the security, privacy, confidentiality, or integrity of the information that its cameras or other devices transmit."[24]

Consumer privacy organizations, such as EPIC, have said that "[o]ne of the primary risks that internet users will face as the Internet of Things expands is the fact that the ubiquitous collection and storage of data about users can reveal sensitive behavior patterns." EPIC cites as an example the potential that a smart power grid's tracking of a consumer's energy use could "reveal intimate, personal details about [consumers'] lives, such as their medical needs, interactions with others, and personal habits."[25]

The debate over IoT parallels in many ways those concerning other developing technology issues, including Big Data and Biometrics. Issues of data collection and use, the role of the government, individual control, ownership of data, and transparency are likely to be actively debated in coming years and may affect the application of current laws or prompt passage of legislation.[26]

---

[22] Andy Greenberg, *Hackers Reveal Nasty New Car Attacks – With Me Behind the Wheel*, FORBES, Aug. 12, 2013, http://www.forbes.com/sites/andygreenberg/ 2013/07/24/hackers-reveal-nasty-new-car-attacks-with-me-behind-the-wheel-video/.

[23] Tarun Wadhwa, *Yes, You Can Hack A Pacemaker (And Other Medical Devices Too)*, FORBES, Dec. 6, 2012, http://www.forbes.com/sites/singularity/2012/12/06/ yes-you-can-hack-a-pacemaker-and-other-medical-devices-too/.

[24] Press Release, Federal Trade Commission, *Marketer of Internet-Connected Home Security Video Cameras Settles FTC Charges It Failed to Protect Consumers' Privacy*, Sept. 4, 2013, http://www.ftc.gov/opa/2013/09/trendnet.shtm.

[25]*Comments of the Electronic Privacy Information Center to The Federal Trade Commission on the Privacy and Security Implications of the Internet of Things*, 10-11, June 1, 2013, http://ftc.gov/os/comments/internetthingscomments/00011-86154.pdf.

[26] *See Bracy supra* n. 19.

11

Privacy and Data Security in Action

Privacy and data security present practical challenges for both businesses and consumers. The complex network of US federal and state laws, the broad authority of the FTC to enforce promises made in privacy and security policies, the federal government's power to compel companies to turn over private information, inconsistent international privacy laws, self-regulatory standards, and guidelines promulgated by governments and standard-setting bodies are part of the background against which privacy stakeholders must operate today. When the dangers of unauthorized incursions into personal and proprietary information and potential liability for businesses, including fines, lawsuits, and regulatory actions are added, it is more than ever necessary to take a proactive and holistic approach to managing privacy and security risks.

Although no "one size fits all" solution exists, several approaches that may prove of value to enterprises are establishing appropriate privacy policies and frameworks, privacy and security audits, training personnel, "privacy by design," establishing appropriate organization and oversight, and managing vendors and third parties. In addition, organizations should closely monitor technological and legislative trends to be prepared to modify their privacy and security policies and practices as new developments arise.

Privacy and Data Protection Infrastructure

The risks that entities face in the privacy and security fields, including lawsuits, regulatory actions, and loss of private and proprietary information, have led senior management and boards of directors to pay increased attention to proper organization of their security and privacy infrastructure. A 2012 report from Corporate Board Member and FTI Consulting found for the first time that data security is the top risk concern for both directors and general counsel, ahead of issues such as operational risk, company reputation, disaster recovery, and global business expansion.[1]

Businesses are increasingly establishing a specialized organizational infrastructure to manage privacy and security, including C-Suite positions responsible for coordinating privacy and security programs. Members of the security and privacy team may include a chief security officer (CSO), sometimes called a chief information security officer (CISO), who is responsible for the entire security program, as well as a chief privacy officer (CPO) responsible for the privacy program.

The CSO and CPO have specialized responsibilities for their respective fields and work in close conjunction with others, including the organization's chief information officer (CIO) and chief risk officer (CRO).[2] Because of the potential liability of corporations and boards of directors described above in Chapter 6, executives in the CSO and CPO positions in some organizations are subject to oversight by the CEO or CFO, as well as by committees of the board of directors, including the risk committee.

A 2012 study by the Carnegie Mellon CyLab found that, despite the advances in developing corporate infrastructures to handle privacy and security risks, boards of directors are still "not actively addressing cyber risk management" and that there remains a large gap "in understanding the linkage between information technology (IT) risks and enterprise risk management."[3] Among the report's findings are that boards and senior management have not established key privacy and security personnel or

---

[1] Corporate Board Member, *Legal Risks on the Radar*, 2, 2012, http://www.fticonsulting.com/global2/media/collateral/united-states/legal-risks-on-the-radar.pdf.
[2] *See* JODY R. WESTBY AND JULIA H. ALLEN, GOVERNING FOR ENTERPRISE SECURITY (GES) IMPLEMENTATION GUIDE (Software Engineering Institute, Aug. 2007).
[3] *See* Jody R. Westby, *Governance of Enterprise Security: CyLab 2012 Report: How Boards & Senior Executives are Managing Cyber Risks*, 5-6, May 16, 2012, http://www.information week.com/whitepaper/Security/Attacks-Breaches/carnegie-mellon-cylab-governance-of-enterprise-se-wp1344272794.

have created combined positions that are not consistent "with internationally accepted best practices and standards."[4]

The report recommended that businesses:

- Establish a risk committee on the board of directors and recruit directors with security and IT governance experience;
- Ensure that privacy and security roles within the organization are separate and that they report separately to senior management;
- Establish a cross-organizational team on privacy and security issues;
- Review policies to "create a culture of security and respect for privacy;"
- Ensure that security and privacy policies conform to best practices;
- Ensure that vendors follow an organization's privacy and security requirements;
- Conduct an annual audit of the organization's security program to be reviewed by the organization's audit committee;
- Conduct an annual review of the organization's security program to be reviewed by the organization's risk committee;
- Require regular reports from senior management on privacy and security risks;
- Require annual board review of budgets for privacy and security risk management;
- Conduct annual privacy compliance audits and test incident response, breach notification, disaster recovery, and crisis communication plans; and
- Assess cyber risk and potential loss valuations and adequacy of cyber insurance coverage.[5]

Privacy and Security Policies and Procedures

Among the best practices that a company should consider adopting are developing internal written policies and procedures governing privacy and

---

[4] *Id.*
[5] *Id.* at 8.

security. These policies should include a general policy or framework for an enterprise's privacy program, as well as more specific privacy and security policies for specific aspects of collection, processing, storing, and other aspects of personal data.

Policies and procedures, including a privacy framework, are not only a best practice, but may be required by law. Federal laws, such as HIPAA and GLB, require written procedures—a requirement bolstered by SOX's mandate that executives properly oversee the security of data environments. For brokers, dealers, and others, the SEC Safeguards Rule also requires adoption of "written policies and procedures that address administrative, technical, and physical safeguards for the protection of customer records and information."

The policies and procedures a business puts in place must be appropriate to its operations and tailored to the relevant national and international regulatory environments. Policies may include those governing:

- Use, access, and retention of consumer reports about hiring or other employment decisions;
- Privacy and security of protected health information under HIPAA;
- Privacy and security of nonpublic personal information under GLB;
- Confidentiality, security, and integrity of information relating to children under COPPA;
- Data breach notification requirements and a plan to respond to a data breach incident;
- Legal requirements for collection, retention, and security of personal information;
- Confidentiality and restrictions on use of social security numbers;
- Social media use by employees;
- Bring Your Own Device (BYOD) policies;
- Ownership and use of social media accounts by employees;
- Transfer of information to or from other countries, including policies incorporating the US/EU Safe Harbor Principles;
- Encryption of personal information in transfer or at rest;
- Protection of customer records and information under the SEC Safeguards Rule;

- Compliance with Payment Card Industry Data Security Rules (PCI DSS);
- Written identity theft prevention programs to comply with the US Red Flags Rule; and
- Proper use by employees of technology, including remote access technologies, laptops, tablets, and e-mail usage.

Companies also should educate their personnel to promote a culture of compliance with laws, standards, and best practices. The PCI DSS require that personnel be educated about security policies upon hire and at least annually to ensure that "key security processes and procedures [are not] forgotten or bypassed, resulting in exposed critical resources and cardholder data." PCI DSS also recommend that personnel acknowledge in writing or electronically applicable policies at least annually to "ensure that they have read and understood the security policies/procedures, and that they have made and will continue to make a commitment to comply with these policies."[6]

Privacy Policies

Most companies have developed privacy policies to provide notice to consumers and others about the company's data collection, use, management, and disclosure policies. Privacy policies are typically part of a user agreement, particularly for online enterprises. Some of the federal laws described in Chapter 2 require privacy policies, including COPPA, GLB, and HIPAA.

Some states have also enacted legislation that affects privacy policies. California's Online Privacy Protection Act (CalOPPA) requires an operator of a commercial website or online service that collects personally identifiable information through the Internet about California consumers to "conspicuously post its privacy policy on its Web site, or in the case of an operator of an online service, make that policy available [by a reasonably accessible means]"[7] The California attorney general has

---

[6] *See* Payment Card Industry (PCI) Security Standard, *Navigating PCI DSS v. 2.0*, 57, Oct. 2010, https://www.pcisecuritystandards.org/security_standards/documents.php.
[7] Ann. Cal. Bus. & Prof. Code §§ 22575-79 (West).

issued guidelines for privacy policies and put developers of mobile applications on notice that they must comply with this law.[8]

CalOPPA requires that the privacy policies of operators identify the categories of personally identifiable information they collect about individual consumers who use or visit their sites and the categories of third parties with whom they share personal information.[9] It also requires an operator to state whether it maintains a process for consumers to request changes to personal information collected on the Web, describe the process by which the operator notifies consumers regarding "material changes" to the privacy policy, and identify the policy's effective date.[10]

CalOPPA was recently amended to also require operators of sites to explain in their privacy policies how they respond to browser do not track (DNT) signals "or other mechanisms that provide consumers the ability to exercise choice regarding the collection of personally identifiable information about an individual consumer's online activities over time and across third-party Web sites or online services, if the operator engages in that collection."[11] The amendment also requires operators to "[d]isclose whether other parties may collect personally identifiable information about an individual consumer's online activities over time and across different Web sites when a consumer uses the operator's Web site or service."[12] As discussed in Chapter 10, compliance with these new requirements, which go into effect on January 1, 2014, may pose difficulties for some operators.

Privacy policies are important because businesses may become targets of regulatory action if they lack such a policy, do not follow their policy, or change the policy without informing consumers. As discussed in Chapter 7, the FTC has brought actions against companies, including Myspace and Facebook, for failing to follow their privacy policies. The California

---

[8] *See* Cal. A.G.'s Office, *Privacy on the Go: Recommendations for the Mobile Ecosystem*, Jan. 2013, http://oag.ca.gov/sites/all/files/pdfs/privacy/privacy_on_the_go.pdf.
[9] Ann. Cal. Bus. & Prof. Code § 22575(b)(1) (West).
[10] *Id.* at § 22575(b).
[11] Assembly Bill No. 370 (Cal. 2013) (amending Cal. Bus. & Prof. C. § 22575(b)(5)), approved by the Governor on September 27, 2013.
[12] *Id.* (amending Cal. Bus. & Prof. Code § 22575(b)(6)).

attorney general has also brought legal actions against companies for failing to have privacy policies in place in violation of CalOPPA.

In addition, regulators worldwide are focusing on privacy policies. The "first-ever online privacy sweep carried out by 19 data protection authorities around the globe" in 2013 revealed that 21 percent of websites had no privacy policy available, a third of the privacy policies had readability problems, and that there were many problems with policies that contained irrelevant information, were difficult to find, and had confusing or no contact information.[13] Failure to follow privacy policies has also served as the basis for civil lawsuits against companies, as discussed in Chapter 8.

Because privacy policies should be tailored to a business' specific practices, there are no hard and fast rules for the content of the policies. In drafting, it should be kept in mind that a privacy policy is a communication to consumers with legal ramifications. Businesses should therefore consider consulting an experienced legal professional both for drafting and for significant revisions of the policy.

It also may be advisable to have a layered privacy policy that provides a general statement about privacy and then allows a user to click on the sections to learn more about the policy. An example of such a layered policy is Microsoft's, which provides general summaries of policies for topics such as cookies, information collected, protection of personal information, children, and display of advertising that link to more detailed information.[14] Businesses should also not adapt another company's privacy policies to their own, given the considerable differences that may exist in the ways in which data is collected, maintained, and processed by companies.

Despite these provisos, privacy policy best practices include:

- An explanation of how a company collects and uses personal information, including cookie policies, sharing customer information, and contact information;

---

[13] Allison Grande, *Many Sites Lack Adequate Privacy Policies, Regulators Find*, LAW 360, Aug. 13, 2013, http://www.law360.com/articles/464601/many-sites-lack-adequate-privacy-policies-regulators-find.
[14] Microsoft.com, *Privacy Statement*, http://www.microsoft.com/privacystatement/en-us/core/default.aspx.

- Prominent display on a website of the company's privacy practices;
- How significant changes in the privacy policy are communicated;
- Publication of any opt-out policies, such as those for e-mail communications; and
- A description of whether the website deals with any regulated information, such as collecting information from children under the age of thirteen.

In drafting privacy policies, it is also advisable not to use language that may come back to haunt a business, such as the company uses "state-of-the art" security practices.[15]

Businesses should make privacy policies comprehensible to consumers. Privacy policies have been often criticized for their lack of readability, complexity, and transparency. As one satirical website states, if the "legal mumbo jumbo" were eliminated from most companies' privacy policies, a privacy policy would say, "we will track and log everything we can about all the dirty (and clean) things you do and like with cookies, GPS, secure collections or whatever technology exists today or becomes available at any time in the future" and that "you may think of using any of our programs or services as the privacy equivalent of living in a webcam fitted glass house under the unblinking eye of Big Brother: you have no privacy with us."[16]

Privacy policies are a likely subject for future federal or state legislation. A member of the 2013 California legislature, for example, proposed a bill that privacy policies "be no more than 100 words and shall be written in clear and concise language at no greater than an eighth grade reading level. The privacy policy shall include a statement indicating whether the personally identifiable information may be sold or shared with others, and if so, how and with whom the information may be shared."[17]

---

[15] *See* Eric Goldman, *Privacy Policies in the United States Presentation Slides*, Technology & Marketing Law Blog, Feb. 6, 2013, http://blog.ericgoldman.org/archives/2013/02/privacy_policie.htm.
[16] *See* Skipty.com, *We are the Company that Cares about Your Privacy*, http://www.skipity.com/privacy/.
[17] Assembly Bill No. 242 (Cal., Feb. 6, 2013), an Act to amend Section 22575 of the Business and Professions Code.

Although the bill itself may have been written at greater than an eighth grade reading level, it clocked in at an admirable seventy-four words.

Privacy and Security Audits

The risks of potential privacy and security issues grow exponentially if an entity does not understand what data it is collecting and creating, where the data is stored, how (and by whom) the data is processed, the ways in which data is destroyed or deleted, and how (and to whom) the data is distributed. In addition, a business should assess on an ongoing basis whether it is compliant with applicable laws and standards. For these reasons a business should consider engaging in regular privacy and security audits, or if it has not done so already, perform a baseline privacy and security assessment.

The details and scope of any privacy or security audit (and whether it is conducted internally or by outside consultants) depend upon the nature of the enterprise involved and the extent of its operations. In some instances, an internal self-assessment of privacy and security controls may be sufficient, particularly if a business collects and maintains a limited range of information. In other cases—particularly where there are risk or compliance issues—audits are better conducted by outside professionals. Consideration should also be given to involving lawyers in an audit if there are potential attorney-client privilege issues that may arise.

For an audit to be effective, management, operational and technical personnel, including the CSO, CPO, CIO, their staffs, and other relevant personnel should be directly involved. Management "buy-in" to privacy and security programs and audits is important, given the risks that companies confront in these areas, including potential legal liability and regulatory scrutiny.

The basic purpose of privacy and security audits, whatever the size of the entity, is to determine whether appropriate procedures and controls are in place to protect privacy and protect information from unauthorized access. Privacy and security audits may thus often lead to remedial measures and improvements, as well as changes in policies and procedures, and may also be useful in demonstrating compliance with applicable regulatory and legal standards.

Among the issues that may be addressed in a privacy audit are:

- Business operation context and any applicable legal requirements, such as GLB or HIPAA;
- Nature of personal and other information gathered by the business and the sensitivity of the data;
- Whether information is subject to regulatory controls and/or disclosure;
- Flow of data within and without the organization, including to third parties;
- Sources of data, and whether data is transferred from or to other jurisdictions such as the European Union;
- Consent issues for processing specific types of sensitive personal data, including social security numbers or credit card data;
- Permitted uses of data;
- Ways in which data is collected, aggregated or anonymized;
- Cookie use;
- Length of time data is stored;
- Ways in which an entity provides users a means to opt-out from collection or distribution of information;
- Permissible disclosures of data to third parties and their use of data;
- Provisions for data accuracy and correction of data; and
- Compliance with privacy policies.[18]

Security audits assess whether a company's security measures are sufficient to withstand unauthorized incursions that can lead to the loss of personal and proprietary information. Security audits are technical in nature and are addressed to the company's specific system architecture. One possible approach to a security audit is to determine whether the "Twenty Critical Security Controls for Effective Cyber Defense" developed by international

---

[18] Keith P. Enright, *Privacy Audit Checklist*, Berkman Center for Internet & Society available at http://cyber.law.harvard.edu/ecommerce/privacyaudit.html.

government experts and promulgated by the SANS Institute are in place to defend networks and systems against internal and external threats.[19] The current version of these critical controls requires:

- Inventory of authorized and unauthorized devices;
- Inventory of authorized and unauthorized software;
- Secure configurations for hardware and software on mobile devices, laptops, workstations, and servers;
- Continuous vulnerability assessment and remediation;
- Malware defenses;
- Application software security;
- Wireless device control;
- Data recovery capability;
- Security skills assessment and appropriate training to fill gaps;
- Secure configurations for network devices such as firewalls, routers, and switches;
- Limitation and control of network ports, protocols, and services;
- Controlled use of administrative privileges;
- Boundary defense;
- Maintenance, monitoring, and analysis of audit logs;
- Controlled access based on the need to know;
- Account monitoring and control;
- Data loss prevention;
- Incident response and management;
- Secure network engineering; and
- Penetration tests and red team exercises.

Vendors and Third Parties

Management of vendors and third parties, including outsourcers, contractors, consultants, cloud computing providers, and business partners, is critical for maintaining a business' privacy and security policies. Without adequate safeguards for the ways in which third parties treat private information and security, an organization's own policies and procedures may be useless.

---

[19] *See* SANS Institute, *20 Critical Security Controls-Version 4.1*, http://www.sans.org/critical-security-controls/.

Because third parties are a frequent source of data breaches, it is particularly important to monitor and control their adherence to required policies and procedures, as well as industry best practices.[20]

Businesses should use due diligence in selecting and retaining vendors, cloud computing providers, and other third parties. Depending upon the nature of the relationship and the third party involved, due diligence may address the security procedures followed by the third party, maintenance of confidentiality and privacy of data, indemnification of the business for any losses incurred, and insurance maintained by the third party.

Contracts with third parties, such as vendors and cloud computing providers, should seek to ensure compliance with privacy and security measures and appropriately allocate risk. After such third parties are engaged, businesses should consider putting in place a vendor management program to monitor performance of vendors, ensure that they follow privacy and security standards, and determine whether insurance and risk management requirements are being followed. If a vendor is discharged or a contract ends, businesses should make sure that all data is returned and that the vendor has appropriately disposed of data.

Privacy by Design

Privacy by design is a means by which a business may "embed[] privacy into information technologies, business practices, and networked infrastructures, as a core functionality, right from the outset..."[21] Privacy by design, which is one of the three major principles of the FTC's 2012 privacy framework, means that "[c]ompanies should promote consumer privacy throughout their organizations and at every stage of the development of their products and services."[22] As framed by the FTC, privacy by design includes

---

[20] *See* Grant Thornton, *Managing Data Security and Privacy Risk of Third-Party Vendors*, http://www.grantthornton.com/staticfiles/GTCom/Health%20care%20organizations/HC%20-%20managing%20data%20-%20FINAL.pdf.

[21] Ann Cavoukian, *Operationalizing Privacy by Design: A Guide to Implementing Strong Privacy Principles*, 8, Dec. 2012, http://www.ipc.on.ca/images/Resources/operationalizing-pbd-guide.pdf.

[22] Federal Trade Commission, *Protecting Consumer Privacy in an Era of Rapid Change: Recommendations for Businesses and Policymakers* 22-3, Mar. 2012, [hereinafter FTC 2012 Report], http://ftc.gov/os/2012/03/120326privacyreport.pdf.

building in privacy protections for data security, reasonable collection limits, sound retention and disposal practices, and data accuracy. Privacy by design also seeks to establish "comprehensive data management procedures throughout the life cycle of [companies'] products and services."[23]

European data protection authorities have also endorsed privacy by design for operating system and device manufactures and for mobile applications. Providing safeguards for data and privacy users includes "ensuring the availability of appropriate mechanisms to inform and educate the end user about what the apps can do and what data they are able to access, as well as providing appropriate settings for app users to change the parameters of the processing."[24]

The originator of these principles, Dr. Ann Cavoukian, has conducted many studies about the applicability of privacy by design principles to businesses, including the use of surveillance cameras in mass transit systems, biometrics in casinos, mobile devices, remote home health care, and big data and data analytics.[25] To pick one possible application of the principles, privacy by design may be incorporated into website architecture through user-experienced design (UXD). Using these principles, matters of importance to the user, such as user interfaces, may be constructed from the outset to protect privacy.[26]

Cybersecurity Insurance

Facing security risks, companies have turned to cybersecurity insurance. Cybersecurity insurance is a type of insurance policy designed to mitigate losses from incidents such as data breaches, network damage, and cyber extortion. Cybersecurity insurance is typically one of several components of an organization's risk management strategy for information security. The

---

[23] *Id*.at 30.
[24] Article 29 Data Protection Working Party, *Opinion 02/2013 on Apps on Smart Devices*, 11, Feb. 27, 2013, http://ec.europa.eu/justice/data-protection/article-29/documentation/opinion-recommendation/files/2013/wp202_en.pdf.
[25] *See Cavoukian supra* n. 21 at 55-58.
[26] Timothy J. Toohey, *Designing for Privacy & Web Success*, WEBSITE MAGAZINE, Jan. 18, 2013, http://www.websitemagazine.com/content/blogs/design-development/archive/2013/01/18/designing-for-privacy-amp-web-success.aspx.

government has also recently initiated studies and reports about the availability of such insurance as part of a broader approach to cybersecurity risks.[27]

The increased threat of cybersecurity attacks and availability of insurance has led to 31 percent of companies having such security policies and 39 percent of companies planning to buy them in the future. The key findings of a recent report about cybersecurity insurance is that companies are motivated by the potential multi-million dollar losses from security incidents in purchasing insurance, and that protecting against insurance cyber risks now ranks high or higher than other insurable risks, such as natural disasters and fires.[28]

As with any insurance policy, companies considering adoption of a cybersecurity policy should consult professionals to determine the appropriate levels of coverage and the types of risks insured.

---

[27] *See* Department of Homeland Security, *Cybersecurity Insurance*, http://www.dhs.gov/pub lication/cybersecurity-insurance; White House Blog, Aug. 6, 2013, *Incentives to Support Adoption of the Cybersecurity Framework*, http://www.whitehouse.gov/blog/2013/08/06/ incentives-support-adoption-cybersecurity-framework.

[28] Ponemon Institute, *Managing Cyber Security as a Business Risk: Cyber Insurance in the Digital Age*, 1, Aug. 7, 2013, http://www.experian.com/innovation/business-resources/pone mon-study-managing-cyber-security-as-business-risk.jsp?ecd_ dbres_cyber_insurance_study_ponemon_referral.

Conclusion

Businesses and consumers in the United States confront many privacy paradoxes that will continue to affect the development of law and best practices. We share private data more readily and for many more purposes than at any time in history. Yet many of us have contradictory attitudes toward this practice, including about what we are willing to share and with whom it is shared.

The growth of social media sites, such as Facebook, video sharing sites, like YouTube, free e-mail services, like Gmail, and other sites, such as Twitter, readily allow us to post large amounts of information about ourselves for public consumption. These sites also make it possible for us to share information with people that we barely know and to find out information about others we may or may not want to know. The information posted or distributed on these sites or through other means, such as text messages, may come back to haunt some of us, as seen in some criminal and civil trials and in many well-publicized incidents involving celebrities and politicians, including Anthony Weiner and Amanda Bynes.[1]

The sharing of information on the Internet may not trigger a privacy response until there are concrete consequences, such as a negative job decision. The privacy implications of social media have become something of a popular culture meme, as seen in a recent "Dilbert" cartoon. In the cartoon, the "Pointy-Haired Boss" tells a job applicant that instead of seeing a resume "we use data from the Internet to see what you've been up to lately." After the boss looks him up online, the applicant beats a quick retreat with the boss remarking, "You'll understand if I don't shake your hand."[2]

---

[1] There are many articles where Facebook evidence was used at trial. *See, e.g.,* Tom McGee, *Facebook Evidence OK for Trial of Man Charged with Threats*, DENVER POST Jan. 4, 2013, http://www.denverpost.com/ci_22308348/facebook-evidence-ok-trial-man-charged-threats; Jim McElhatton, *Feds use Facebook to Collect Crime Evidence*, WASH. POST Apr. 27, 2011, http://www.washingtontimes.com/news/2011/apr/27/feds-use-facebook-to-collect-crime-evidence/?page=all.

[2] Dilbert, Sept. 5, 2013, http://www.dilbert.com/2013-09-05/.

But there is also the contradictory evidence that most of us have taken measures to protect our personal information. A September 5, 2013 survey on *Anonymity, Privacy, and Security Online* conducted by the Pew Internet Project found a remarkable 86 percent of Internet users had taken steps "to remove or mask their digital footprints – ranging from clearing cookies to encrypting their e-mail."[3] When asked who they were trying to avoid by doing this, 33 percent responded "hackers or criminals," 28 percent "advertisers," 19 percent "certain friends," 19 percent "people from your past," 17 percent "people who might criticize/harass you," and 14 percent "family members or romantic partner." Interestingly, only 5 percent replied they were trying to avoid the government and 4 percent law enforcement.[4]

Commenting on the conclusions of the study, the director of the project said that "[p]rivacy isn't an all-or-nothing kind of proposition. For many people, it depends on what kind of data is at issue; it depends on who is traditionally watching; it depends on what they think the consequences are, and maybe it even depends on what stage of life they're at. It's all conditional and all contextual. It's not 'I want full full full privacy' or 'I want everyone to know everything.'"[5]

The implications of the privacy paradox for those attempting to craft policies and procedures is that privacy and sharing personal information will continue to be a double-edge sword. Eager to share or even "overshare," consumers also want to protect their privacy. Because of the continuum of attitudes toward privacy, the law is likely to continue to be unsettled. As a practical matter, businesses must therefore accommodate themselves to uncertainty and "expect the unexpected" as privacy law continues to evolve.

---

[3] Pew Internet Project, *Anonymity, Privacy, and Security Online*, 2, Sept. 5, 2013, http://pewinternet.org/~/media//Files/Reports/2013/PIP_AnonymityOnline_090513.pdf.
[4] *Id.* at 5.
[5] Angelique Carson, *Survey: Users More Afraid of Peers than Gov't When It Comes to Data Access*, IAPP Privacy Advisor, Sept. 6, 2013, https://www.privacyassociation.org/publications/survey_users_more_afraid_of_peers_than_govt_when_it_comes_to_data_access.

Further Reading

I found these sources of importance in researching and preparing this book.

- FRED H. CATE, PRIVACY IN THE INFORMATION AGE (Brookings Institution Press, 1997).
- PRIVACY PROGRAM MANAGEMENT: TOOLS FOR MANAGING PRIVACY WITHIN YOUR ORGANIZATION (Russell R. Densmore, ed., 2013).
- JONATHON D. AVILA, ET AL., PRIVACY COMPLIANCE AND LITIGATION IN CALIFORNIA (Continuing Education of the Bar – California, 2012).
- ANDREW B. SERWIN, INFORMATION SECURITY AND PRIVACY: A GUIDE TO FEDERAL AND STATE LAW AND COMPLIANCE (LegalWorks, 2013).
- INFORMATION SECURITY AND PRIVACY: A PRACTICAL GUIDE FOR GLOBAL EXECUTIVES, LAWYERS AND TECHNOLOGISTS (Thomas J. Shaw, ed., 2011).
- DANIEL J. SOLOVE, UNDERSTANDING PRIVACY (Harvard University Press 2008).
- EUROPEAN PRIVACY: LAW AND PRACTICE FOR DATA PROTECTION PROFESSIONALS (Eduardo Ustaran, ed., 2012).

In addition to the above, I recommend that anyone interested in the field check out the resources provided by the International Association of Privacy Professionals (IAPP), https://www.privacyassociation.org/, including its invaluable "Daily Dashboard" of news stories about privacy and data security.

Frequently Asked Questions

Q: **What is Data Privacy?**

A: Data privacy has many definitions, but it is essentially the right or claim of individuals, groups, or institutions to determine for themselves when, how, and to what extent information about them is communicated to others.

Q: **What is Personal Data?**

A: Personal data can be defined both generally and specifically. Generally, personal data may be defined as any information relating to an identified or identifiable natural person. More specifically, personal data may include first and last name, addresses, online contact information, user names, passwords, telephone numbers, social security or identification card numbers, persistent identifiers, geolocation information, photographs or video files with images, and many other categories of data.

Q: **What are the Fair Information Practice Principles?**

A: The Fair Information Practice Principles (or FIPPs) are basic principles of notice, choice, access, and security relating to personal data.

Q: **Are the Fair Information Practice Principles binding or enacted into a specific law?**

A: The Fair Information Practice Principles have served as a basis for some sectoral federal laws, including the Privacy Act and the Children's Online Privacy Protection Act (COPPA), but they are not embodied in any federal baseline privacy law in the US. They continue to serve as a basis for proposals for laws for consumer privacy rights, including proposals in 2012 by the Federal Trade Commission (FTC) and the White House.

Q: What role does self-governance or self-regulation play in US privacy and security law?

A: Self-governance plays an important role in the US because there is no baseline privacy law. Unlike the European Union (EU), which does have a baseline privacy law, the US relies on a patchwork quilt of federal and state laws. In the absence of comprehensive laws, companies frequently adopt protections for privacy and security implemented through internal procedures and privacy policies. Companies may also follow contractually required standards and voluntary standards promulgated by third parties, such as the Digital Advertising Alliance's self-regulatory programs for online behavioral advertising (OBA).

Q: What protection does the US Constitution provide for privacy?

A: The US Constitution does not mention the word privacy, but the Fourth Amendment protects the "right of the people to be secure in their persons, houses, papers, and effects, against unreasonable searches and seizures..." The US Supreme Court has found that the Fourth Amendment protects a "reasonable expectation of privacy." The Fourth Amendment applies only to the government and not to private parties, but it does impact more general discussions of privacy in the US.

Q: What is the Privacy Act?

A: The Privacy Act is a federal law that establishes fair information practices for personal information systems maintained by the federal government. It has been applied narrowly and has many exceptions and exemptions. There is a private right of action under the Privacy Act.

Q: What is the Fair Credit Reporting Act (FCRA)?

A: FCRA is a federal law that ensures that consumer reporting agencies exercise their responsibilities for the collection and dissemination of consumer credit information with fairness, impartiality, and a respect for the consumer's right to privacy. It is enforced by the FTC and by a private right of action. It applies not only to consumer credit reports, but to reports obtained by employers hiring or taking other actions in regard to existing or prospective employees.

Q: What is the Health Insurance Portability and Accountability Act of 1996 (HIPAA)?

A: HIPAA is a federal law establishing national standards for health care. It contains Privacy and Security Rules that have a significant impact on the protection of health information. For example, the Privacy Rule limits the permitted disclosure of "protected health information." The Security Rule establishes national security standards for protecting health information held or transferred in electronic form. HIPAA is enforced by the Office for Civil Rights (OCR) of the US Department of Health and Human Services. There is no private right of action under HIPAA.

Q: What is the Gramm-Leach-Bliley Act (GLB)?

A: GLB is a federal financial services modernization law that includes rules relating to financial privacy and security. GLB requires financial institutions to provide privacy notices to consumers and customers explaining their information sharing practices. Customers have the right to limit sharing of some, but not all, of their nonpublic personal information. GLB's "Safeguards Rule" requires financial institutions to secure and maintain the confidentiality of nonpublic personal information. GLB is enforced by the FTC, financial industry regulators, and state attorney generals. There is no private right of action under GLB.

Q: What is the Children's Online Privacy Protection Act (COPPA)?

A: COPPA is a federal law regulating the online collection of information from children less than thirteen years old. The primary purpose of the law, according to the FTC, is to "place parents in control over what information is collected from their young children online." The law applies to operators of websites and mobile apps "directed" to children under thirteen years old. The law requires operators to adhere to specific rules, including obtaining verifiable parental consent before collecting information from children. COPPA is enforced by the FTC. There is no private right of action under COPPA.

Q: What is the Computer Fraud and Abuse Act (CFAA)?

A: CFAA is a federal law that makes it a crime to intentionally access a computer without authorization or to exceed authorized access. It is enforced as a criminal law by the US government and also confers a private right of action.

Q: What is the Electronic Communications Privacy Act (ECPA)?

A: ECPA is a federal law that extends wiretapping protections to transmission of electronic data. It includes the Wiretap Act, which addresses the interception of communications, and the Stored Communications Act (SCA), which governs communications at rest. It is enforced by the US government and also confers a private right of action.

Q: Have the individual states in the US enacted laws affecting privacy and security?

A: Individual states have enacted laws affecting many areas of privacy and security. The laws are not consistent with one another and may pose compliance issues for companies operating in multiple states.

Q: What types of laws have the states enacted?

A: States have enacted laws addressing, among other matters, the privacy of medical information, privacy of consumer information, privacy of credit and credit cards, privacy of social security numbers, invasion of privacy and call monitoring, and the privacy of minors. California has been the most active state in some of these areas of legislation.

Q: Do privacy laws outside the US differ from those in this country?

A: Privacy laws in other countries differ considerably from those in the US. Many of these laws are more comprehensive and proscriptive than the laws in the US, which typically apply only to certain types of information or industries.

Q: Does the European Union (EU) have a privacy law?

A: The current law that governs privacy is the European Data Protection Directive of 1995 also known as the "Directive." It is based on the premise that privacy in the EU is a fundamental right. The Directive has a broad definition of personal information. Among other things, it requires data "controllers" only to process data under specific requirements, including a data subject's consent, compliance with legal obligations imposed on the controller of the data, protection of the data subject's vital interests and for purposes of the "legitimate interests" pursued by the data controller.

Q: What is a "data protection authority" (DPA) in the EU?

A: A DPA is an authority or official in a EU member state that has power to enforce the Directive with complete independence. Under some circumstances, DPAs must be notified and approve data processing activities and be informed about data breaches. DPAs also have investigative and enforcement authority regarding the Directive.

Q: Does the Directive affect transfer of personal data from the EU to the US?

A: The Directive prohibits transfer of personal data from EU member states to other countries unless those countries "ensure[] an adequate level of data protection." The US is not considered to have an "adequate level of data protection."

Q: How do companies transfer data from the EU to the US?

A: Several mechanisms exist to allow transfer of data. One of these mechanisms is the EU/US Safe Harbor. By joining this voluntary program and adhering to its principles, US businesses are deemed to have "adequate" privacy protections. The seven "Safe Harbor Principles" are notice, choice, onward transfer, access, security, data integrity, and enforcement. The FTC and the Department of Transportation enforce the Safe Harbor.

Q: What is the EU's proposed new privacy law?

A: The EU has proposed a data privacy regulation that would apply uniformly to all of the EU member states. Its terms are currently being debated in the EU. Although there is no final text for the law, the proposed regulation would affect a broader range of companies than the Directive, tighten the conditions for consent of data processing, establish a single regulatory authority for compliance, a uniform mechanism for enforcement and fines, and establish a "right to be forgotten" – erasure of personal data when an individual withdraws consent, objects to processing personal data, and when data is no longer necessary or there is no legitimate reason for a company to keep the data.

Q: What other countries have privacy laws?

A: Many countries have privacy laws including, among others, Canada, Mexico, Australia, Hong Kong, Singapore, Korea, and South Africa. The laws often differ from one another and from US laws.

Q: What types of legal issues arise from the use of social media in the workplace?

A: Numerous issues have arisen, including employers asking employees to disclose usernames and passwords, mixed personal and work uses of social media sites, and issues involving discussions by employees about employers on sites.

Q: What is BYOD?

A: BYOD is an abbreviation for "Bring Your Own Device." Instead of providing employees with a device, some businesses allow them to access business applications from their own devices, including smartphones. BYOD has led to issues involving security of a company's proprietary and confidential information, as well as privacy issues, including potential access by employers to personal information on employee devices.

Q: How does data security differ from data privacy?

A: Data security refers to securing information against unauthorized access, attack, or loss. Data security protects not only personal, but also proprietary and other valuable information against hackers, malware programs, phishing, and other malicious incursions. Security is necessary to protect privacy and may be described as a means towards that goal.

Q: What laws apply to data protection and security in the US?

A: Numerous laws apply on the federal level, including the HIPAA Security Rule, the GLB Safeguards Rule, COPPA, the Sarbanes Oxley Act (SOX), and rules issued by the US Securities Exchange Commission (SEC). In addition, President Obama in 2013 issued an Executive Order addressing cybersecurity for the country's critical infrastructure. Laws on cybersecurity have also been proposed in Congress.

Q: Are there any state laws that apply to data protection and security?

A: Almost all states have data breach notification laws and some states have laws mandating that data be kept secure or encrypted under some circumstances.

Q: What is a data breach notification law?

A: A data breach notification law typically requires a business to disclose the breach of security of a system to a state's residents when unencrypted personal data is believed to have been acquired by an unauthorized person. Personal information includes information such as social security or identification numbers, medical information, account numbers, and passwords. Information about breaches may also have to be submitted to state authorities, such as a state attorney general. Some states, including California, also require that the breach notice contains specific information relating to the breach.

Q: **Do state data breach notification laws differ?**

A: State data breach notification laws differ in several respects. Some states, including California, do not require any threshold for harm to trigger the notification obligation. Other states, such as Ohio and Pennsylvania, require notice only if there is a reasonable belief that the breach will cause harm, such as identity theft. Laws also differ as to their definition of personal information, whether notification is required for paper records, and the content of the notice.

Q: **May businesses be held liable for a data breach even if they have been victimized by an attack?**

A: Government authorities may take actions against businesses for security failures. Among the agencies that have brought such actions are the OCR for HIPAA violations, the FTC for violations of the GLB Safeguards Rule and Section 5 of the FTC Act, and the SEC. Other potential sources for liability include shareholder derivative suits alleging that a corporation failed to follow corporate law and direct shareholder actions alleging that security breaches have decreased the share price of the company's stock.

Q: **How does the FTC enforce privacy laws?**

A: The FTC has authority to enforce thirty-three federal privacy provisions including COPPA, FCRA, GLB, the Red Flags Rule and EU-US Safe Harbor. The FTC also has power to enforce privacy and data security under Section 5 of the FTC Act.

Q: **What is the FTC's authority under Section 5 of the FTC Act?**

A: The FTC has authority to investigate and prevent businesses from engaging in "unfair methods of competition in or affecting commerce, and unfair or deceptive acts or practices in or affecting commerce." Under the unfairness prong of Section 5, the FTC focuses on consumer injury as a result of unfair practices. Under the deception prong, the FTC focuses on representations, omissions and practices that mislead or are likely to mislead consumers.

Q: Has the FTC brought actions involving privacy and data security under Section 5?

A: The FTC has brought numerous privacy and security complaints under Section 5, including complaints against Google, Myspace, Facebook, and Twitter. The FTC fined Google $22.5 million in 2012 for violating an order by misrepresentations concerning Apple's Safari browser. The FTC has also brought actions against companies that have allegedly misrepresented their security measures protecting consumers' personal data.

Q: Can private plaintiffs bring lawsuits for privacy claims?

A: Privacy litigation is quite common in the US. In recent years, class action lawsuits have been brought against many prominent companies, including AOL, Facebook, Apple, and Google.

Q: Have plaintiffs been successful in these actions?

A: Plaintiffs have had some success in these actions, but have also faced challenges. The challenges include the lack of standing under Article III of the US Constitution, the inability to show injury in fact (damages) for personal data and the difficulty of fitting the facts of the case into a legal theory. Courts have thrown out many privacy litigations, but actions are currently proceeding against several prominent companies.

Q: What is "Big Data"?

A: Big Data is not a precise term, but it generally refers to the ability to sort and organize massive amounts of unstructured data from multiple sources in a short period of time. Big Data may also mean the ability to find patterns or results from large amounts of data or to data sets so large that they cannot be handled by traditional database tools.

Q: What privacy and security concerns are associated with Big Data?

A: Among other matters, privacy advocates have cited the potential loss of control by consumers, lack of transparency, lack of legal accountability, and the increased security risks of Big Data as concerns.

Q: What is "Cloud Computing"?

A: Cloud computing is a colloquial term that refers to the storage or processing of data in a location other than the user's computer system. Software and storage services are typically managed by a third party called a "cloud computing provider." Cloud computing is used as part of a distributed business model to increase flexibility and scalability, lower costs, and allow access from multiple locations or devices. Apple's iCloud and Google Apps for Business are examples of cloud computing.

Q: What privacy and security concerns are associated with Cloud Computing?

A: Issues may arise when there is a breach of privacy or security as to whether the client or the hosting party is responsible for data stored on the cloud. Other issues include restrictions on the transfer of data imposed by some countries, such as the EU member states.

Q: What is "Do Not Track" (DNT)?

A: DNT is a proposed http header built into Internet browsers to ask a website to disable its tracking of a consumer for advertising purposes. The White House and the FTC have endorsed DNT as promoting privacy and consumer choice.

Q: What are Biometric Identifiers?

A: Biometric identifiers are unique physiological traits of human beings used for identification, authentication or security purposes. Common biometric identifiers include fingerprints, DNA, iris scans, voice identification, and keyboard strokes. Some find biometric identifiers controversial because of the perceived invasion of the privacy of the bodily features of a person.

Q: **What is the Internet of Things (IoT)?**

A: IoT consists of machines and other devices with sensors or chips that send data to the Internet. IoT includes "smart" devices such as mobile telephones, cars, appliances, power meters and medical devices. Privacy and security concerns relating to IoT include the potential misuse of data, hacking of devices, and revealing sensitive behavior patterns from collection and storage of data.

Q: What is a Privacy Policy?

A: A privacy policy is a notice provided by a company to consumers about its data collection, use, management and disclosure policies. Privacy policies are typically posted online or provided in conjunction with a user agreement. Privacy policies track a company's internal policies and procedures and may be required by law. Some companies that have not followed their privacy policies have been targets of regulatory action by the FTC.

Q: What is a Privacy Audit?

A: A privacy audit is an audit that addresses the manner in which a business collects, retains, processes, and destroys personal information. An audit may address any applicable legal requirements, the nature of the data gathered by the business and its sensitivity, the flow of data within the organization and to third parties, sources of data, restrictions on transfer of data, consent issues, permitted uses of data, compliance with privacy policies, and numerous other matters.

Q: What is a Security Audit?

A: A security audit assesses whether a company's security measures are sufficient to withstand unauthorized incursions that can lead to the loss of personal and proprietary information. Security audits are technical in nature and are addressed to a company's specific system architecture.

Q: What is "Privacy by Design"?

A: Privacy by design is a means by which a business incorporates privacy into information technologies, business practices, and networked infrastructure as a core functionality from the outset. The concept was pioneered by Dr. Ann Cavoukian and has been endorsed by the FTC and EU authorities.

Q: What is cybersecurity insurance?

A: Cybersecurity insurance is a type of insurance policy designed to mitigate losses from incidents such as data breaches, network damage and cyber extortion. It is typically a part of an organization's risk management strategies.

ABOUT THE AUTHOR

Timothy J. Toohey is a partner with the Los Angeles law firm of Morris Polich & Purdy LLP and head of the firm's Cyber, Privacy and Data Security team. Mr. Toohey is a United States Certified Information Privacy Professional (CIPP/US) and a European Union Certified Information Privacy Professional (CIPP/E). His practice concentrates on privacy and data protection matters, as well as intellectual property and technology litigation.

Mr. Toohey has handled a variety of privacy and data protection matters, including advice and litigation regarding the Computer Fraud and Abuse Act, the US/EU Safe Harbor, the Fair Credit Reporting Act (FCRA), the Health Information Portability and Accountability Act (HIPAA), the Children's Online Privacy Protection Act (COPPA), the Electronic Communications Protection Act (ECPA), the Stored Communications Act (SCA) and other privacy and data protection laws. He has also been involved in numerous matters involving state law, including matters arising under California's Song-Beverly Act, the California Medical Information Act (CMIA), the California Invasion of Privacy Act (CIPA), the California Online Privacy Protection Act (CalOPPA), and state data breach notification laws. Mr. Toohey has also dealt with international privacy and security issues, including compliance with European Union data protection and privacy directives and the proposed EU data protection regulation.

Mr. Toohey's experience includes trial and arbitration of trademark, design patent, and copyright infringement matters, as well as licensing and trade secret disputes. He has been involved in several high profile anti-counterfeiting and infringement cases for consumer products and intellectual property matters involving the entertainment industry.

Mr. Toohey has spoken and written widely on privacy, data security, technology, and intellectual property matters. Among his recent publications are *The Balance Between Data Flow and Privacy: A United States Perspective* which appeared in the JOURNAL OF LAW AND ECONOMIC REGULATION and *Piracy, Privacy, and Internet Openness: The Changing Face of Cyberspace Law*, which was published in INSIDE

THE MINDS: UNDERSTANDING DEVELOPMENTS IN CYBERSPACE LAW, 2012 ED. by Aspatore Books, a Thomson Reuters business. Mr. Toohey has written op-eds on privacy issues for USA TODAY and other publications, and is frequently quoted in major national publications on data and security issues.

Mr. Toohey is a member of the Community Outreach Advisory Board of the Information Systems Security Association (ISSA), Los Angeles Chapter. He has also lectured in the UCLA Department of History, where he teaches courses in United States Constitutional and Legal History.

Mr. Toohey received his JD from Boalt Hall School of Law, University of California, Berkeley and has a PhD in history from Harvard University. He attended Stanford University and Wadham College, Oxford University as a Rhodes Scholar.

Mr. Toohey's work in the cyber, privacy, and data security fields may be followed through his website: www.privacydatasecurity.com, his LinkedIn profile: http://www.linkedin.com/pub/timothy-toohey/14/824/457, and through Twitter: @tj2e.

INDEX

ASPATORE